Country Entertaining

TIME-LIFE BOOKS

Alexandria, Virginia

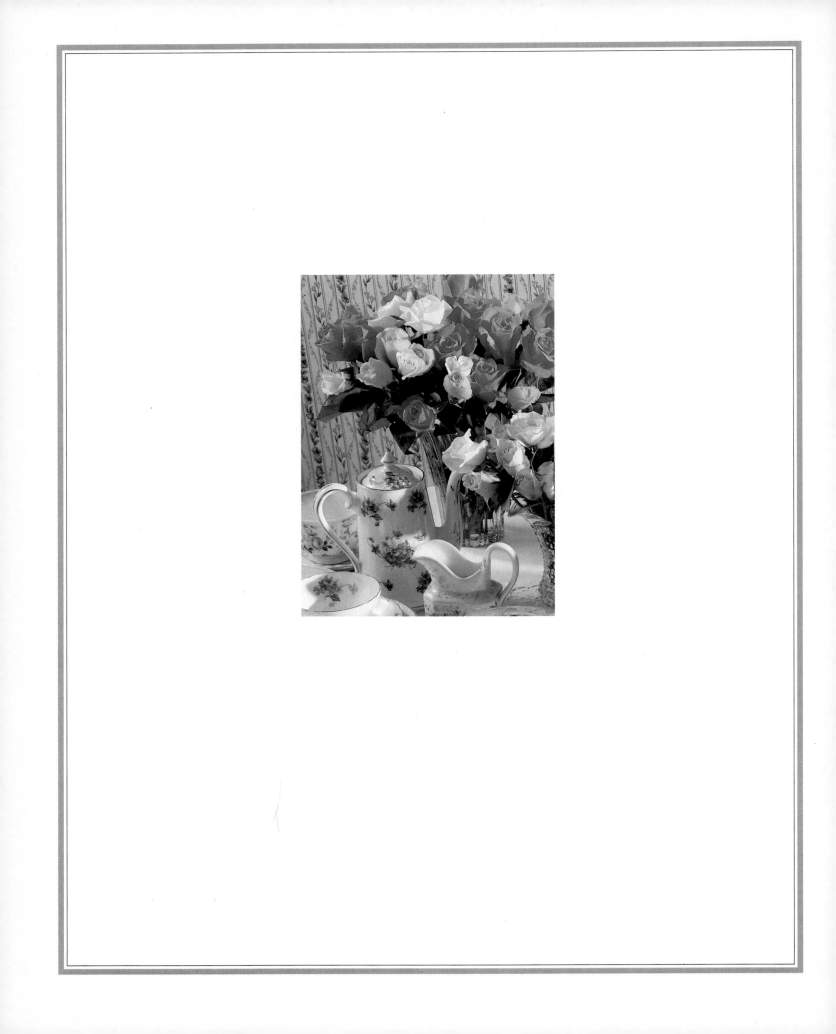

Country Entertaining

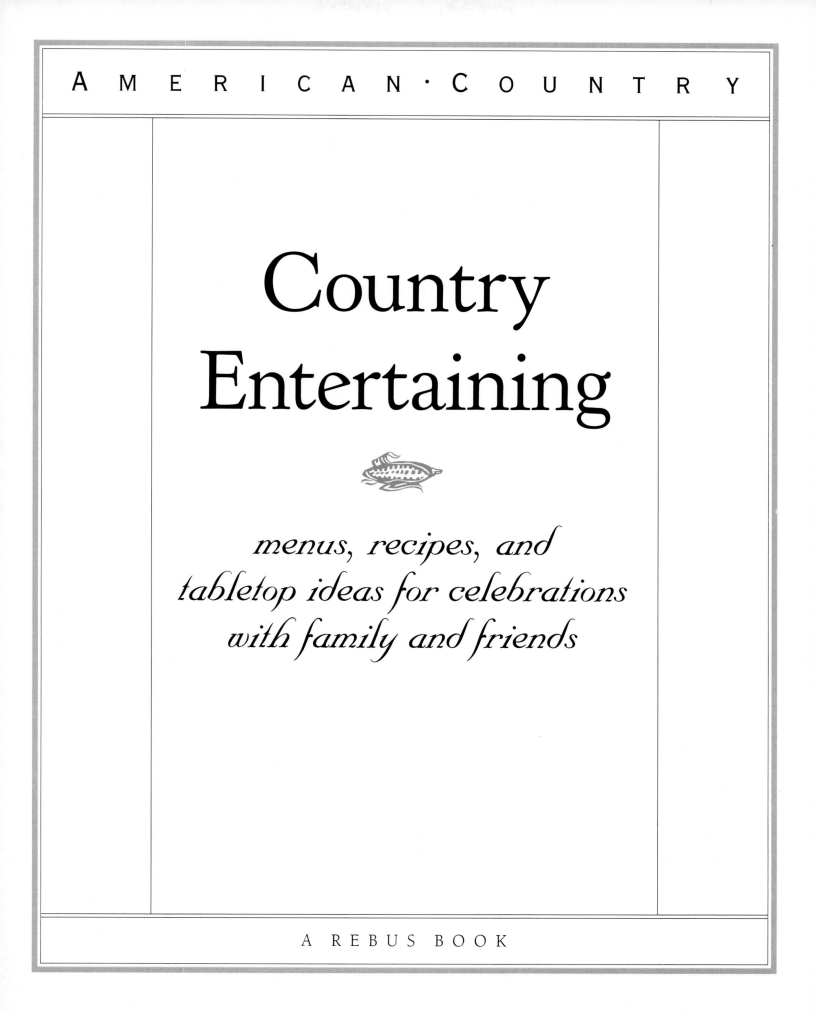

*menus, recipes, and
tabletop ideas for celebrations
with family and friends*

A REBUS BOOK

CONTENTS

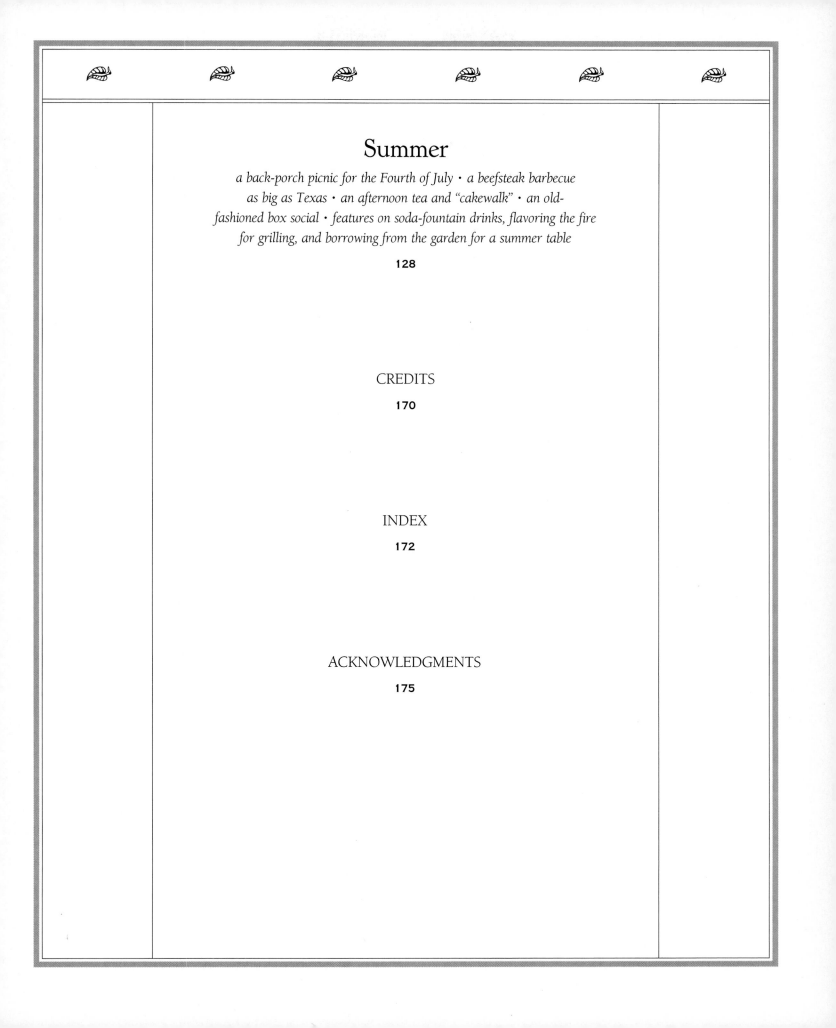

Summer

*a back-porch picnic for the Fourth of July · a beefsteak barbecue
as big as Texas · an afternoon tea and "cakewalk" · an old-
fashioned box social · features on soda-fountain drinks, flavoring the fire
for grilling, and borrowing from the garden for a summer table*

128

Americancountry entertaining has always followed the seasons. In earlier times, the changing weather and the garden calendar inspired gatherings such as the harvest supper, apple-butter bee, and strawberry festival. Today, we can still honor such seasonal occasions in the spirit of country hospitality.

The tradition of fresh foods, lovingly prepared and served in comfortable surroundings, remains at the heart of country entertaining. In her *Handbook of Hospitality for Town and Country*, published in 1909, Florence Howe Hall observed that a hostess should "provide her guests the best products of the countryside—fresh fruit, vegetables and eggs, chickens that have never darkened the door of the cold-storage warehouse, cream and milk that have never traveled by train." Today, country- and city-dwellers alike have access to a wealth of fine ingredients, which can be easily elevated to honest but gracious "company" status. For example, on the following pages you will learn to stuff a chicken with lemons and roast it to a turn; grill baby vegetables with a touch of oil and herbs; bake crisp apples or meltingly ripe persimmons into a pie or cake; and transform milk, cream, and eggs into luxuriously rich pecan ice cream.

The dinners, suppers, picnics, and parties described in this volume take much of their inspiration from bygone days, but also respect the contemporary palate. Following the cycle of the seasons, the chapters embrace major holidays as well as more personal celebrations. The menus are flexible: Most can be adapted to serve any number of guests. In addition, many of the dishes will work well with more than one menu. Keep in mind that you can always add a special flourish, such as a bottle of wine from a local vineyard, a sprinkling of fresh garden flowers in a salad, or a table decoration you've crafted yourself.

Indeed, it is when setting the scene for a festive meal that you can truly express your personal tastes. Casual country entertaining lends itself to spontaneous touches: Gather an armful of daisies to place in a pretty pitcher, or fill a favorite bowl with red-blushed pears. For more formal occasions, take the extra time to set an elegant table with your best china and linens and, perhaps, a special centerpiece.

Whether you live in town or country, the recipes and entertaining ideas in this book will help you to host comfortable, convivial gatherings for the people you care about most. Above all, be sure to take time to relax and enjoy your guests. For as Ralph Waldo Emerson once wrote, "The ornament of a house is the friends who frequent it."

Autumn

*a time for giving
thanks for nature's
bounty*

Although there is a certain poignancy to summer's end, autumn brings with it the celebration of the harvest. Moreover, the arrival of vibrant foliage heralds the appearance of crackling-crisp apples and juicy pears, succulent grapes, and a sustaining store of squashes and root vegetables. As the weather turns brisk, thoughts turn to the warmth of hearth and kitchen, where hot, hearty meals restore the spirit.

Informal autumn activities—visiting a country farmstand, attending a hometown football game, or lighting a fire on the first cool evening—can become occasions for companionable gatherings where fall foods like chili, mulled cider, and squash pie are certain to be welcome. And Thanksgiving, the season's most festive holiday, allows ample opportunity for enjoying such perennial favorites as pumpkins, cranberries, and pecans.

In autumn, apples and pumpkins, squashes and corn please both eye and palate.

FALL FARMSTAND
SUPPER

Mulled Cider

Vermont Cheddar Spread • Crackers

New England White Bean Soup

Savory Stuffed Squash

Golden Pumpkin Bread • Apple-Pear Butter

Gingered Apple-Cranberry Sauce

Autumn Brown Betty

Maple-Butternut Squash Pie

SERVES 6

▼

An autumn excursion to a roadside farmstand, orchard, or farmer's market is the starting point for this all-day gathering. Invite some friends along for the country marketing trip, then have them join you for a convivial afternoon of cooking followed by a well-earned meal. Heat the cider and mix the cheese spread first, so that you can snack on them while cooking. Prepare the soup and stuffed squash next (to be reheated later), then choose which of the side dishes and baked goods to make—or make them all, if your crew is energetic. By suppertime, the house will be redolent of autumn's spicy scents. If your kitchen is too small for group cooking, prepare the meal yourself and invite friends to join you afterward for a harvest celebration.

Mulled Cider

If the apple cider you buy appears crystal clear, it has been filtered and possibly pasteurized to preserve it. As long as the cider is vacuum sealed in a glass bottle, it can be kept at room temperature. Once opened, it will keep for up to a week in the refrigerator. "Natural" cider, which has more of the fruit pulp left in, is a cloudy golden brown. It should be kept refrigerated; even chilled, it will begin to ferment, or turn "hard," after a few days. Either type of cider is fine for this recipe. If cider is not available, use apple juice. For a slightly alcoholic drink, add a little applejack or apple brandy to each mug of mulled cider before you serve it.

10 whole cloves
3 small cinnamon sticks, plus additional
*   sticks for garnish (optional)*

1 gallon apple cider
2 lemons, sliced, plus additional slices for
*   garnish (optional)*

    1. Place the cloves and 3 of the cinnamon sticks in a double thickness of cheesecloth, fold it into a packet, and fasten it with string.
    2. Pour the cider into a large pot, add the spice packet and the 2 sliced lemons, and bring to a simmer. Simmer the cider for 30 minutes; do not let it boil.
    3. Ladle the cider into mugs. Garnish with additional cinnamon sticks or lemon slices, if desired.

Makes 16 cups

Whether you're storing or serving it, the sharp, tangy Vermont Cheddar Spread can be packed into old-fashioned canning jars or stoneware pots. Dressed with a ribbon bow, a container of the cheese blend makes a lovely gift.

Vermont Cheddar Spread

A fine, well-aged Vermont Cheddar will give a sharp, zesty flavor to this spread. However, a New York State, Wisconsin, or other domestic Cheddar—or an imported English cheese—will also yield a tasty appetizer. The cheese mixture can be made ahead of time, but should be served at room temperature for best flavor. As an accompaniment, offer sturdy crackers such as the so-called "common" crackers, once found in every New England general store; thick and crunchy, they look like little biscuits. Any other firm crackers—or raw vegetable sticks—can be substituted.

1 package (3 ounces) cream cheese,
*   softened to room temperature*
4 tablespoons butter, softened to room
*   temperature*

½ pound sharp white Cheddar cheese, grated
3 tablespoons chopped fresh chives
½ teaspoon dry mustard
Pinch of cayenne pepper

    1. In a medium bowl, using an electric mixer, beat the cream cheese and butter until well blended. Beat in the Cheddar until blended.
    2. Add the chives, mustard, and cayenne, and beat until fluffy. Transfer the mixture to a crock or bowl. Cover and refrigerate until ready to serve.

Makes about 1¾ cups

New England White Bean Soup

One of the luxuries of weekend cooking is having the time to prepare dishes that require long, slow cooking, such as this flavorful soup. Two hours of simmering on the stove renders the beans soft and creamy, and extracts every bit of goodness from the ham hock. If you make the soup ahead of time—which will further improve its flavor—refrigerate it and skim the fat before reheating.

1 pound dried navy or Great Northern
   beans, rinsed and picked over
2 tablespoons vegetable oil
1 medium onion, coarsely chopped
2 cloves garlic, minced
2 medium carrots, diced (about 1 cup)
2 stalks celery, diced (about 1 cup)
2 medium white turnips (about 1 pound),
   peeled and diced

8 cups canned chicken broth, preferably low-
   sodium
1 smoked ham hock (about ¾ pound)
1 teaspoon thyme
½ teaspoon pepper
1 bay leaf
¼ cup chopped parsley

1. Place the beans in a large soup pot with water to cover by 2 inches. Bring to a boil and boil for 2 minutes. Remove from the heat, cover, and let stand for 1 hour.

2. Meanwhile, in a medium skillet, heat the oil over medium heat. Add the onion, garlic, carrots, celery, and turnips, and sauté until softened, about 5 minutes; remove the skillet from the heat and set aside.

3. Drain the beans and return them to the soup pot. Add the chicken broth, ham hock, thyme, pepper, and bay leaf. Stir in the sautéed vegetables. Bring the mixture to a boil over medium-high heat, then reduce the heat to medium-low and simmer, covered, until the beans are tender, about 2 hours.

4. Discard the bay leaf. Remove and discard the ham hock. Alternatively, if you wish to include the ham in the soup, trim the meat off the ham hock and cut into bite-size pieces. Return the meat to the pot, and reheat briefly. Stir in the parsley and serve hot.

6 servings

A tureen in the shape of a stout head of cabbage or a plump pumpkin is fine for serving the white bean soup. To help keep the contents warm, fill the tureen with boiling water and let stand briefly, then empty it and ladle in the soup.

Savory Stuffed Squash

Almost any variety of hard-shell squash—green or golden acorn, butternut, or buttercup—could be used for this recipe. Sweet-fleshed miniature pumpkins would also make a very appealing presentation; cut the tops off, rather than cutting the pumpkins in half. Other autumn favorites, such as bell peppers or eggplant halves, can be stuffed in the same manner, but the cooking time will be shorter for softer vegetables.

The author of a 1909 entertaining manual told of a country friend whose pleasure it was to have neighbors drop in to take potluck with her. "This young matron . . . does not leave her guests alone in the parlor. She makes what she calls A KITCHEN PARTY where everybody helps, and work is turned into good fun. . . . it is wonderful how people enjoy following the lead of a merry hostess!"

3 acorn or other hard-shell squash (about 3 pounds total)
1 tablespoon butter
1 medium onion, coarsely chopped
3 cloves garlic, minced
1 cup cottage cheese
1 cup grated Swiss cheese

½ cup fresh whole-wheat breadcrumbs
4 tablespoons chopped parsley
1 egg, lightly beaten
1 teaspoon oregano, crushed
½ teaspoon salt
½ teaspoon pepper

1. Preheat the oven to 350°. Line a baking sheet with aluminum foil.

2. Using a large, heavy knife, cut each squash in half lengthwise. Place the squash halves, cut-side down, on the foil-lined baking sheet and bake for 30 minutes, or until the thickest part is just tender when pierced with a knife. Set aside to cool slightly. Increase the oven temperature to 375°.

3. While the squash is cooling, make the stuffing: In a medium skillet, melt the butter over medium heat. Add the onion and garlic, and cook until translucent, about 5 minutes; set aside to cool slightly.

4. Stir in the cottage cheese, ½ cup of the Swiss cheese, the breadcrumbs, 2 tablespoons of the parsley, the egg, oregano, salt, and pepper; set aside.

5. Scoop out the seeds and fibers from the squash halves, then scoop out and reserve just enough of the flesh to leave a ½-inch-thick shell. Cut the reserved flesh into bite-size pieces and add it to the stuffing.

6. Return the squash shells, cut-side up, to the baking sheet and divide the stuffing evenly among them. Sprinkle the tops with the remaining ½ cup Swiss cheese and bake for 15 minutes, or until the stuffing is heated through and the cheese is melted and bubbly. Sprinkle the remaining 2 tablespoons parsley over the cheese, and serve.

6 servings

Savory Stuffed Squash, New England White Bean Soup, and Gingered Apple-Cranberry Sauce

Golden Pumpkin Bread

If you prefer to use fresh pumpkin for this recipe, halve and seed a 1½-pound pumpkin; cut it into small pieces and peel them. Steam the pumpkin pieces for 15 to 20 minutes, or until tender, then mash them or put them through a food mill.

1½ cups flour
½ cup yellow cornmeal
1 teaspoon baking powder
1 teaspoon cinnamon
1 teaspoon ground ginger
1 teaspoon nutmeg
½ teaspoon salt

1 stick (4 ounces) butter, softened to room
   temperature
⅔ cup sugar
2 eggs
1 cup canned unsweetened pumpkin
1 cup chopped pecans
1 cup raisins

1. Preheat the oven to 350°. Grease and flour a 9 x 5-inch loaf pan.

2. In a medium bowl, stir together the flour, cornmeal, baking powder, cinnamon, ginger, nutmeg, and salt.

3. In a large bowl, cream the butter and sugar. Beat in the eggs one at a time, beating well after each addition. Stir in the pumpkin until thoroughly combined, then gradually add the dry ingredients, beating just until incorporated; do not overbeat. Stir in the pecans and raisins.

4. Spread the batter evenly in the prepared pan. Rap the pan once or twice on the counter to remove any air pockets. Bake for 50 to 60 minutes, or until the bread shrinks from the sides of the pan and a toothpick inserted in the center of the loaf comes out clean and dry.

5. Let the loaf cool in the pan on a rack, then turn it out to cool completely before slicing.

Makes one 9-inch loaf

Golden Pumpkin Bread and Apple-Pear Butter

Apple-Pear Butter

This is an updated version of a traditional apple-butter recipe, which requires most of a day for reducing cider and apples down to the proper consistency. Here, apples and pears are simmered until tender, then puréed and cooked for about one hour longer.

*4 Granny Smith or other flavorful apples
    (about 2 pounds)
4 ripe Bartlett pears (about 1½ pounds)
½ cup apple cider*

*1 tablespoon lemon juice
1½ teaspoons cinnamon
½ teaspoon ground cloves
Honey, to taste*

1. Peel and core the apples and pears, then cut them into ½-inch-thick slices.

2. Combine the apples, pears, cider, lemon juice, cinnamon, and cloves in a large nonreactive pot and bring to a boil over medium-high heat. Reduce the heat to medium-low, cover, and simmer, stirring every 15 minutes or so, for 45 minutes.

3. Uncover the pot. Lightly crush with a fork or potato masher any fruit that has not fallen apart. Simmer the fruit, stirring occasionally, until very thick and dark brown, about 1 hour more; be careful not to let the mixture scorch.

4. Add honey. Transfer the mixture to a food processor or blender and process just until puréed. Return the purée to the pot and cook, uncovered, over medium-low heat, stirring frequently, until very thick, about 30 minutes more.

5. Let the apple-pear butter cool to room temperature, then cover and refrigerate until serving time.

Makes about 3 cups

Gingered Apple-Cranberry Sauce

McIntosh, Delicious, and Granny Smith apples are available all year round in most parts of the country, but fresh-picked local apples are one of the great delights of fall. Gravensteins, Jonathans, Rhode Island Greenings, Northern Spies, Newtown Pippins, Winesaps, or Empires would all work well in this recipe.

*5 pounds apples, peeled, cored, and cut
    into large chunks
2 cups fresh or frozen cranberries
¾ cup sugar, or to taste*

*1 tablespoon plus 2 teaspoons grated
    fresh ginger
1 teaspoon cinnamon*

1. In a large saucepan, combine the apples, cranberries, sugar, ginger, and cinnamon, and toss until well mixed. Let stand for 30 minutes, stirring occasionally, until the apples begin to release their juices.

2. Cover the pan, place it over medium heat, and cook, stirring frequently, until the fruit is very soft, about 40 minutes.

3. With a potato masher, gently mash the fruit into a chunky sauce. If the sauce seems watery, cook it, uncovered, for a few more minutes.

Makes about 8 cups

Here is author Della Lutes' description of old-time apple-butter making, from Home Grown: *"Hour after hour the huge kettle swinging on its iron crane . . . steamed and bubbled and stewed, its sweet and spicy aroma scenting all the air; while someone stood . . . swaying the long-handled stirrer back and forth to keep the rich thickening mass from sticking to the sides. In earlier times than ours, they made a 'bee' out of apple-butter time . . . thereby turning labor into an excuse for frolic."*

Autumn Brown Betty

A Brown Betty is usually made with apples and breadcrumbs; this recipe calls for apples and pears, which are layered with graham-cracker crumbs for a toasty whole-wheat flavor. Serve it with vanilla ice cream or lightly sweetened whipped cream.

⅔ cup apple cider
4 medium apples (about 2 pounds),
   peeled and thinly sliced
2 medium pears, peeled and thinly sliced
1 cup golden raisins
⅔ cup (packed) dark brown sugar

2 tablespoons lemon juice
1 teaspoon cinnamon
½ teaspoon ground ginger
1 cup graham-cracker crumbs (8 crackers)
2 tablespoons butter, cut into small pieces

1. Preheat the oven to 350°. Lightly butter a 13 x 9-inch baking pan.

2. In a small saucepan, bring the cider to a boil. Remove the pan from the heat, cover, and set aside.

3. Place the apple and pear slices in a medium bowl, add the raisins, sugar, lemon juice, cinnamon, and ginger, and toss until well mixed.

4. Spread half of the apple mixture in the prepared pan, then top it with half of the graham-cracker crumbs. Make another layer, finishing with the crumbs on top.

5. Pour the hot cider over the crumb-topped fruit mixture, and dot it with the butter. Bake for 60 minutes. Serve hot or warm. *6 servings*

Nearly a century ago, the author of A Handbook of Hospitality for Town and Country *waxed nostalgic about color-themed parties. "The Yellow Supper of our grandmothers . . . deserves to be revived. . . . Early autumn is the proper time for its celebration. The bill of fare should comprise baked pumpkin, sweet corn . . . baked quinces and pumpkin johnnycake. Golden-hued pears and apples make a pretty centerpiece and serve also as dessert."*

Maple-Butternut Squash Pie

Sweetened with pure maple syrup and spiced with ginger and cinnamon, the squash custard filling for this delicately flavored pie is reminiscent of pumpkin pie filling.

PASTRY
1¼ cups flour
¼ cup yellow cornmeal
2 tablespoons granulated sugar
¾ teaspoon salt
7 tablespoons chilled butter, cut into pieces
5 to 6 tablespoons ice water

FILLING AND GLAZE
¼ cup heavy cream
¼ cup (packed) light or dark brown sugar

⅓ cup maple syrup
¾ teaspoon cinnamon
¾ teaspoon ground ginger
3 eggs, lightly beaten
1½ pounds butternut squash, baked, cooled,
   and smoothly mashed (about 2 cups)
¼ cup yellow cornmeal
2 tablespoons butter, melted
¾ teaspoon salt
1 egg yolk beaten with 1 tablespoon milk

1. Make the pastry: In a large bowl, combine the flour, cornmeal, granulated sugar, and salt. With a pastry blender or two knives, cut in the butter until the mixture resembles coarse crumbs.

Maple-Butternut Squash Pie and Autumn Brown Betty

2. Sprinkle 5 tablespoons of the ice water over the mixture and toss it with a fork. The dough should be just barely moistened, enough so it will hold together when it's formed into a ball. If necessary, add up to 1 tablespoon more water. Form the dough into a flat disk, wrap in plastic wrap, and refrigerate for at least 30 minutes.

3. On a lightly floured surface, roll the dough out to a 12-inch circle. Fit the dough into a 9-inch glass pie plate. Trim the overhang to an even ½ inch all the way around and reserve the trimmings. Fold the overhang under and crimp the dough to form a decorative border. Prick the pastry with a fork.

4. Roll out the trimmings and cut out a maple-leaf shape. Mark veins on the leaf with the back of a knife and place the leaf on a sheet of lightly greased foil. Place the pie shell and maple leaf in the freezer to chill for at least 15 minutes before baking.

5. Preheat the oven to 400°.

6. Line the pie shell with foil, fill it with pie weights or dried beans, and bake it for 10 minutes. Remove the foil and weights and set the pie shell aside to cool; reduce the oven temperature to 350°.

7. Make the filling: In a large bowl, combine the cream, brown sugar, maple syrup, cinnamon, and ginger, and stir until well blended. Stir in the beaten eggs, then add the squash, cornmeal, butter, and salt, and stir until blended; set aside.

8. Brush the edge of the pie shell and the top of the maple-leaf cutout with the egg-yolk mixture.

9. Pour the filling into the pie shell and bake it for 50 minutes, or until the crust is golden. Bake the leaf cutout on the foil for the last 30 minutes. Let the pie and the leaf cool to room temperature, then place the leaf on top of the pie.   *Makes one 9-inch pie*

COUNTRY PUMPKINS

It's just not Halloween without a pumpkin—or a whole family of them. As a change from the usual grinning jack-o-lanterns, try "carving" the pumpkins with cookie cutters. Here stars, hearts, moons, leaves, and other shapes were used to produce an eye-catching display.

Take a good look at your pumpkin before deciding how to carve it: its shape may suggest a particular design. If the pumpkin is to be displayed against a wall, leave the back uncut, so that the candlelight is concentrated toward the cut portion.

Start by cutting off a lid—holding the knife at an angle so that the lid will be supported by a beveled ledge—then scoop out the seeds and membranes (save the seeds to toast, if you like). If the pumpkin is small, with a fairly thin shell, you may be able to cut all the way through with a deep metal cookie cutter. However, if the pumpkin is thick walled, you may have to mark the pattern with the cookie cutter (tap it in lightly with a hammer or trace it with a felt-tipped pen) and then finish cutting with a sharp paring knife. Check the kitchen and garage for other useful implements: An apple corer, for example, makes clean, coin-size cuts, while punches or large nails make smaller, even-size holes.

When the carving is done, place a stout candle on an inverted metal jar lid (secure the candle with a drop of melted wax) and place it inside the pumpkin. Then wait until dark, light the candle, and enjoy your unique Halloween handiwork.

CHILI FEAST

Seven-Vegetable Chili • Southwestern Chili

Three-Alarm Chili

Buttermilk-Squash Cornbread

Cinnamon-Apple Sundaes

SERVES 12 TO 15

▼

This meal is perfect for a sports-loving group: Serve it after a hometown football game or while watching the World Series. It also makes an easy housewarming or open-house buffet. There's plenty of food for hearty appetites, and with three chilies—a mild vegetable chili, a spicier beef-and-pork Tex-Mex version, and a seriously hot beef chili—there's something for every taste. Each bowlful can be further "personalized" with extras such as sour cream, shredded Monterey Jack or Cheddar cheese, lime wedges, mashed avocado, shredded lettuce, grated carrots, cut-up tomatoes, and sliced radishes and cucumbers.

The chilies and cornbread can be prepared a day in advance, so that at party time you need only reheat the chili on the stove and freshen the bread in the oven. You can also make the ice-cream sauce ahead of time; just warm it up and arrange the ice cream, sauce, and cookie topping as a serve-yourself sundae bar.

Seven-Vegetable Chili

To make the most efficient use of your time, set the dried pinto beans aside to soak while you begin to prepare the Southwestern and Three-Alarm chili recipes. When the other two chilies are simmering on the stove, drain the pinto beans and continue with this recipe. As a further timesaver, you could make this dish with canned beans: Use 3⅓ cups of beans, rinsed and drained. For a truly vegetarian chili, substitute vegetable broth or water for the chicken broth.

A Mexican menu is not difficult to carry out," advised a turn-of-the-century party guide. "Tamales, frijoles and several sweetmeats are kept by all first-class grocers, and other dishes may be prepared by recipes that have been modified to suit the untried American palate."

1½ cups dried pinto beans
4 tablespoons oil
1 medium red onion, coarsely chopped
   (about 1 cup)
4 cloves garlic, minced
2 cups cauliflower florets
1 medium sweet potato, peeled and diced
1 large green bell pepper, diced
2 large carrots, diced
3 cups corn kernels, fresh or frozen

1 can (35 ounces) whole tomatoes, with
   their juice
1 cup canned chicken broth
3 tablespoons ground cumin
3 tablespoons chili powder
2 tablespoons tomato paste
2 teaspoons paprika
1½ teaspoons salt
⅛ teaspoon cayenne pepper
¼ cup chopped fresh coriander

1. Place the beans in a large saucepan with water to cover by 2 inches. Bring to a boil and boil for 2 minutes. Remove from the heat, cover, and let stand for 1 hour.

2. Drain the beans, add fresh water to cover, and bring to a boil. Reduce the heat to low and simmer, covered, until the beans are tender, 45 minutes to 1 hour; drain and set aside.

3. In a Dutch oven or flameproof casserole, heat 2 tablespoons of the oil over medium heat. Add the onion and garlic, and sauté until the onion is softened but not browned, about 10 minutes.

4. Add the remaining 2 tablespoons oil to the pan, then add the cooked, drained beans, the cauliflower, sweet potato, bell pepper, carrots, corn kernels, tomatoes with their juice, broth, cumin, chili powder, tomato paste, paprika, salt, and cayenne, and stir until well combined. Bring to a boil over medium-high heat, then reduce the heat to medium-low and simmer, covered, stirring frequently, until the vegetables are just tender, about 10 minutes. For more tender vegetables, cook the chili for up to 20 minutes longer.

5. Just before serving, stir in the coriander.   *Makes about 12 cups*

Seven-Vegetable Chili

Southwestern Chili

Ground pork and chunks of beef in a cornmeal-thickened broth make this the heartiest chili on the menu. To prepare it ahead of time, follow the directions through Step 3, then cover the pot and refrigerate the mixture. Just before serving, bring it to a boil and then continue with Step 4.

2 tablespoons olive oil
2 pounds stew beef, cut into bite-size
   pieces
2 pounds ground pork
2 cups chopped scallions (about 10)
12 cloves garlic, minced
About 5 cups canned beef broth
2 cans (4 ounces each) diced mild green
   chilies, drained

⅔ cup chopped fresh coriander, plus fresh
   coriander sprigs, for garnish (optional)
½ cup chili powder
¼ cup ground cumin
1 tablespoon oregano, crushed
⅛ teaspoon cayenne pepper
⅔ cup yellow cornmeal
Salt and black pepper

1. In a Dutch oven or flameproof casserole, heat the oil over medium-high heat. Add the beef and pork, and sauté until lightly browned, about 8 minutes.

2. Reduce the heat to low. Transfer the cooked meat to a bowl, reserving the fat in the pan. Sauté the scallions and garlic in the fat until softened, about 10 minutes.

3. Return the meat to the pan and stir in 3 cups of the broth, the green chilies, chopped coriander, chili powder, cumin, oregano, and cayenne. Bring to a boil, reduce the heat to low, and simmer, covered, stirring occasionally, until the meat is tender, about 2½ hours. Add more broth (up to 1 cup) as necessary to keep the chili from sticking.

4. Fifteen minutes before serving, combine the cornmeal and 1 cup of the remaining broth. Return the chili to a boil over medium heat and stir in the cornmeal mixture. Reduce the heat to medium-low, cover, and simmer, stirring occasionally, until the sauce thickens, about 5 minutes. Season with salt and black pepper to taste, and garnish with coriander sprigs, if using.   *Makes about 10 cups*

Folk art looks fabulous on a country table. These carved and painted coyotes lend an almost audible accent to this Tex-Mex meal. The weathered metal cactus sculpture and rustic ceramic candlesticks add their own Southwestern charm.

Three-Alarm Chili

This beefy dish is truly hot, thanks to the aromatic ancho (the dried form of the poblano chili). The ancho is roughly triangular in shape, with a mahogany-colored skin, and is the dried chili most commonly used in Mexican cooking. A few precautions are necessary when cooking with chilies; see A Primer on Chilies, pages 30-31.

Out of the pantry and onto the table: This colorful assortment of dried beans—including Spanish Tolosanos, Tongues of Fire, Steuben Yellow Eyes, and Cranberry Beans—creates an eye-catching display.

6 dried ancho chilies, seeded

2 cans (14 ounces each) stewed tomatoes, with their juice

1 cup dark beer

1 cup canned beef broth

10 cloves garlic, minced

¼ cup chili powder

2 tablespoons ground cumin

2 tablespoons paprika

2 teaspoons oregano, crushed

1 teaspoon sugar

⅛ teaspoon cayenne pepper

3 tablespoons oil

2 medium onions, coarsely chopped (about 3 cups)

2 pounds beef chuck, cut into ½-inch chunks

¼ cup flour

1. Place the chilies in a small saucepan with cold water to cover and bring to a boil. Cover the pan, reduce the heat to low, and simmer for 15 minutes; remove the pan from the heat.

2. Drain the chilies. In a food processor or blender, combine the drained chilies, tomatoes with their juice, beer, broth, garlic, chili powder, cumin, paprika, oregano, sugar, and cayenne, and process until smooth. Set aside.

3. In a Dutch oven or flameproof casserole, heat the oil over medium heat. Add the onions and sauté until softened but not browned, about 10 minutes.

4. Increase the heat to medium-high, add the beef, and sauté until lightly browned, about 10 minutes. Stir in the flour.

5. Add the tomato mixture to the beef and onions, and stir until well combined. Bring to a boil, reduce the heat to medium-low, and simmer, covered, stirring occasionally, until the beef is very tender, the sauce is thick, and the flavors are well blended, about 2½ hours.

Makes about 9½ cups

Buttermilk-Squash Cornbread

This delicately sweet bread will vary slightly in color and flavor depending on the type of squash you use. Try acorn, butternut, or hubbard squash, or even pumpkin.

2 cups flour
2 cups yellow cornmeal
4 teaspoons baking powder
1 teaspoon baking soda
2 teaspoons salt
2 sticks (8 ounces) butter, softened to
   room temperature

½ cup sugar
2 eggs, lightly beaten
2 cups cooked, mashed winter squash
½ cup buttermilk, or ½ cup milk plus 1½
   teaspoons vinegar

1. Preheat the oven to 350°. Butter and flour two 9 x 5-inch loaf pans.
2. In a medium bowl, stir together the flour, cornmeal, baking powder, baking soda, and salt.
3. In a large bowl, cream the butter and sugar until light. Beat in the eggs, then beat in the squash and buttermilk. Gradually beat in the dry ingredients just until blended.
4. Spread the batter evenly in the prepared pans. Rap the pans on the counter once or twice to remove any air pockets. Bake for 50 minutes, or until a toothpick inserted in the loaves comes out clean and dry. Let the breads cool in the pans on a rack for 10 minutes, then turn them out onto the rack to cool completely.

Makes two 8-inch loaves

I*ce cream is as much the national dish of Mexico as the tortilla," proclaimed a 1904 guide to entertaining. "Mexicans generally eat ice cream before going to bed, but most Americans will find it a pleasant ending for . . . a peppery dinner."*

Cinnamon-Apple Sundaes

Vanilla ice cream is a perfect foil for the autumnal tang of apples and cinnamon in a buttery caramel sauce. Crunchy oatmeal cookies provide a contrast of texture.

1 pound apples, cored,
   halved crosswise, and thinly sliced
4 tablespoons butter
1 cup (packed) light brown sugar

1 tablespoon cinnamon
2 tablespoons heavy cream
1 gallon vanilla ice cream
18 to 20 oatmeal-raisin cookies

1. Place the apples, butter, sugar, and cinnamon in a medium saucepan, and cook over medium-low heat, stirring often, until the sugar is dissolved and the mixture is thick, about 10 minutes.
2. Stir in the cream and cook just until the mixture is the consistency of a caramel sauce, 1 to 2 minutes. Turn off the heat.
3. Scoop the ice cream into dessert dishes and spoon about 2 tablespoons of the sauce over each portion. Reserving one whole cookie per serving, crumble the remaining cookies and sprinkle them over the sundaes.

12 to 15 servings

Cinnamon-Apple Sundaes

A Primer on Chilies

Chilies give an authentic pungency to Tex-Mex and Mexican dishes. Although some chilies are just slightly hotter than bell peppers, others will bring tears to the eyes of the most dedicated hot-food fan.

The fresh chilies shown are just a few of the hundreds of varieties grown. They are listed here from mildest to hottest: The cherry pepper, popular for pickling, is usually quite mild, as is the New Mexican chili, commonly used for *chiles rellenos* (stuffed peppers). Next is the thick-fleshed, aromatic poblano, also used for stuffing, followed by the pale yellow, slightly sweet Santa Fe Grande, which is good in uncooked salsas. Cascabels ("jingle bells") are about as hot as Santa Fes. Chili lovers enjoy fiery jalapeños slivered on nachos or in salsas. Hotter still, pequíns can be added whole during cooking and removed before serving. Cayennes, used to make red pepper flakes, are even hotter, and habaneros (also called Scotch Bonnets) may be the hottest peppers in the world.

Buy firm, plump chilies and refrigerate them wrapped in paper towels, then placed in a loosely closed plastic bag. Some precautions are necessary when preparing chilies: Capsaicin, the substance that gives chilies their heat, can burn your eyes and skin. Wear thin rubber gloves when working with chilies; or handle the chilies under cold running water and wash your hands afterward in warm soapy water or a mild bleach solution. *Never* touch your face — especially your eyes — while handling chilies.

Some chilies are dried to make a long-keeping seasoning. When bought, they should be glossy, not dusty or crumbly; refrigerate them sealed in a plastic bag or container. Despite their more intense flavor, dried chilies can be substituted for fresh, if necessary: Soak them in hot water for about 15 minutes, then seed and devein them. The same precautions apply for dried as for fresh chilies; in addition, be careful not to inhale the powder if you grind dried chilies. The dried varieties included here are, in order of increasing heat: anchos (dried poblanos), pasillas, cascabels, chipotles (dried, mesquite-smoked jalapeños), and japonéses.

You can, to some extent, modify the heat of the chilies when you cook with them. Because the capsaicin is concentrated in the veins and the seed-bearing central core, removing these parts will cool the fire a bit; soaking chilies in cold salted water for an hour will also draw out some of the heat.

Chili peppers are almost too beautiful to cook with. Left to right, top: New Mexican, Santa Fe grande, chipotle, cascabel, and pasilla (dried). Middle: japonés (dried), red and green cherry peppers, red chili, ancho (dried), habanero. Bottom: poblano, dried cascabel, jalapeño, red Portugal.

FIRESIDE SUPPER

Cider-Glazed Fresh Ham

Sautéed Apple Slices

Turnip Purée with Scallion Crisps

Broccoli with Lemon • *Tossed Green Salad*

Pear-Hazelnut Upside-Down Cake

SERVES 6

▼

For the hostess whose home has a fireplace, crisp autumn weather brings many opportunities to share the comforts of the hearth. Take the time to prepare the fire carefully, so that a strong, clear blaze will burn throughout the evening with minimal attention. Welcome your guests into a house filled with the tantalizing aromas of roast ham and autumn fruits and vegetables, then sit down at a table set in front of the fire. Or, serve the supper on trays or tray tables arranged close to the hearth.

A golden pear upside-down cake brings the meal to a delicious close. Spice the after-dinner coffee or tea with cardamom, cinnamon, or cloves, and follow it with a fireside session of charades—or simply good, relaxed conversation. If you don't have a fireplace, enjoy this supper where you can watch the sunset, or just serve it in the coziest corner of your living room, by lamplight or candleglow.

Cider-Glazed Fresh Ham

Fresh ham is the term used for uncured leg of pork. It is cooked the same way as beef or veal, not like cured ham. For this recipe, choose a bone-in ham weighing 6 to 8 pounds. Don't worry if you can only find a larger ham; the leftovers are delicious.

6- to 8-pound fresh ham
1 teaspoon salt
½ teaspoon pepper
24 whole cloves

2 cups apple cider
1 cup dark beer
3 tablespoons brown sugar

1. Preheat the oven to 450°.
2. Trim the outer skin and fat from the ham, leaving ¼ inch of fat around the bone area. Rub the ham with the salt and pepper, and stud it with the cloves.
3. Place the ham on a rack in a roasting pan, put it in the oven, and immediately reduce the oven temperature to 325°. Bake the ham for 15 minutes.
4. Meanwhile, in a small bowl, stir together the cider, ¾ cup of the beer, and the sugar. After the ham has baked for 15 minutes, pour the cider glaze over it. Bake the ham, basting it with the pan juices every half hour, for 4 to 4½ hours, or until a meat thermometer inserted into the ham (not near the bone) registers 170°.
5. Transfer the ham to a platter and let it stand for 15 minutes before carving.
6. Meanwhile, make the gravy: Skim off as much fat as possible from the juices in the roasting pan. Add the remaining ¼ cup beer and place the pan over medium heat, stirring to scrape up the brown bits that cling to the pan. Cook over low heat until hot, about 1 minute.
7. Carve the ham and serve it with the gravy.

6 servings

Robust red wines go well with fall foods. For a festive look, wrap the bottle in a large cloth napkin. First, fold the napkin in half diagonally, then "diaper" the bottle with it. Bring the points around to the front and tie them in a square knot.

Sautéed Apple Slices

Pork and ham are often paired with fruit accompaniments. Here, unpeeled apple slices are sautéed in butter and flavored with nutmeg and brandy. This tasty side dish will bring a touch of color to the meal.

1 Red Delicious apple
1 Golden Delicious apple
2 tablespoons butter

1 tablespoon brown sugar
¼ teaspoon nutmeg
2 tablespoons apple brandy

1. Core and thinly slice the unpeeled apples. In a large nonstick skillet, melt the butter over medium heat. Add the apple slices and cook, stirring, until the apples begin to brown, 2 to 3 minutes.
2. Add the brown sugar, nutmeg, and brandy, and cover the pan. Reduce the heat to low and cook until the apples are just tender, 1 to 2 minutes. Stir the mixture, then serve the apples with pan juices spooned over them.

6 servings

Turnip Purée with Scallion Crisps

Since the oven will be needed for baking the ham until just 15 minutes before serving time, prepare this recipe through Step 3 before putting the ham in the oven. Make the scallion topping (and reheat the turnip purée, if necessary), while the ham rests prior to carving. The batter-fried scallion crisps make a tasty addition to other mashed or creamed vegetables; try them with sweet or white potatoes, carrots, or winter squash.

3 pounds white turnips
1 tablespoon water
⅓ cup butter
3 tablespoons heavy cream
1½ teaspoons salt
½ teaspoon white pepper

⅓ cup yellow cornmeal
⅓ cup flour
1 bunch scallions, cut into 2-inch pieces
   (about 1 cup)
2 eggs, lightly beaten

1. Preheat the oven to 350°.
2. Peel the turnips and cut them into ¼-inch-thick slices. Place the slices in a single layer in a baking pan, sprinkle them with the water, and cover with foil. Bake for 25 to 30 minutes, or until tender when pierced with the tip of a sharp knife.
3. Place the turnips in an ovenproof bowl and mash them with a potato masher until smooth, then stir in 3 tablespoons of the butter, the cream, 1 teaspoon of the salt, and the pepper. Cover the bowl to keep the purée warm.
4. Just before serving, reheat the turnip purée, if necessary.
5. Meanwhile, in a small bowl, stir together the cornmeal, flour, and the remaining ½ teaspoon salt.
6. In a medium skillet, heat the remaining butter over medium heat. Dip the scallions into the beaten eggs, shake them to remove the excess, then roll them in the cornmeal mixture. Fry the scallions in the butter, turning them frequently, until crisp and golden, about 5 minutes.
7. Chop the fried scallions and sprinkle them over the turnip purée.

6 servings

The patterns on your linens, china, and flatware may suggest decorative touches that will help coordinate the tablesetting. Here, the gold cord design of the plate is echoed by lengths of gold drapery cord tied around each napkin.

Pear-Hazelnut Upside-Down Cake

Although usually made with canned pineapple, upside-down cake can be varied with almost any fresh fruit, even berries or bananas. This autumn version has chopped hazelnuts in the batter and is topped with an attractive pinwheel of pear slices. The cake can be baked in a deep 9-inch round cake pan, but it is traditionally prepared in a cast-iron skillet. You can make this cake in any heavy, ovenproof skillet, as long as it has straight, not slanted, sides.

Easy Entertaining by Caroline French Benton, published in 1911, supplied reflections on, and suggestions for, parties in every season. Of an October dinner the author wrote, "Autumn entertaining is of a delightfully informal character, reflecting the life of the summer rather than anticipating that of the winter. This lends the charm of simplicity to both the table and the menu; neither is over-elaborate."

TOPPING
1 large, firm Bartlett pear
2 tablespoons flour
4 tablespoons butter, softened to room
   temperature
⅓ cup sugar
½ cup chopped hazelnuts

CAKE
2¼ cups flour
1¼ teaspoons baking powder
¾ teaspoon baking soda

1½ teaspoons cinnamon
¾ teaspoon ginger
½ teaspoon salt
6 tablespoons butter, softened to room
   temperature
½ cup sugar
3 eggs
½ teaspoon almond extract
¾ cup buttermilk, or ¾ cup milk plus 2¼
   teaspoons vinegar
1 cup chopped hazelnuts

1. Preheat the oven to 350°.

2. Make the topping: Core the unpeeled pear and cut it into ¼-inch-thick slices. Dredge the pear slices in the flour; set aside.

3. In a 9-inch ovenproof skillet with straight sides, melt the butter over medium heat. Add the sugar, and cook, stirring constantly, until the sugar dissolves and the mixture is golden brown, about 4 minutes.

4. Remove the skillet from the heat. Arrange the pear slices, overlapping slightly, in a circular pattern over the sugar mixture and press them down gently. Sprinkle the pears with the hazelnuts; set aside.

5. Make the cake: In a medium bowl, stir together the flour, baking powder, baking soda, cinnamon, ginger, and salt; set aside.

6. In a large bowl, cream the butter until fluffy. Gradually beat in the sugar, then add the eggs, one at a time, and continue beating until the mixture is light and fluffy. Beat in the almond extract.

7. Alternating between the two, add the dry ingredients and the buttermilk, beating well after each addition. Stir in the hazelnuts.

8. Spread the batter evenly over the pear layer. Rap the skillet gently once or twice on the counter to remove any air pockets. Bake for 40 to 45 minutes, or until the cake shrinks from the sides of the skillet and a toothpick inserted in the center of the cake comes out clean and dry.

9. Immediately run the tip of a knife around the edge of the skillet to loosen the cake, then carefully turn it out onto a plate. Serve the cake warm, or at room temperature.

Makes one 9-inch cake

Pear-Hazelnut Upside-Down Cake

FIREPLACE TREATS

A crisp autumn evening is the perfect time for a hearthside party featuring desserts cooked over the fire. A snapping blaze in a country fireplace is a magnet for guests, evoking thoughts of treats such as popcorn and toasted marshmallows. (Sample these desserts only if you burn wood in your fireplace; do not cook over the flames of an artificial log.)

S'mores need no introduction for anyone who has ever been to Scout camp (or attended a backyard barbecue), but the basic recipe—a toasted marshmallow and a piece of chocolate sandwiched between graham crackers—is open to creative interpretation. Try chocolate-coated graham crackers, chocolate wafers, gingersnaps, or brownies instead of plain graham crackers; or add peanut, almond, or cashew butter, or sliced bananas, to the "filling."

Toasted marshmallows have potential beyond S'mores: They become Shaggy Dogs when dipped in melted chocolate and then in shredded coconut. And if you've mastered the delicate art of toasting bread over a fire, sample this slightly more sophisticated creation: Spread a slice of lightly toasted bread with butter and marmalade, then enfold a golden-brown melted marshmallow in the toast.

Popcorn is one of the simplest of fireplace foods: A long-handled popping basket shaken over the fire turns out extremely crisp, toasty-tasting popcorn. To flavor the corn, drizzle it with cinnamon-sugar butter, honey, molasses, or melted chocolate. Or

toss the popcorn with semisweet chocolate chips or grated sweet chocolate and chopped peanuts.

Fresh fruits are unexpectedly delicious when toasted over a fire. Chunks of pineapple, apple, or pear, or whole strawberries, cherries, or fresh figs can be threaded on metal skewers and basted with a mixture of honey and melted butter. Or, sprinkle the fruit with brown sugar, which will caramelize over the fire. Dried fruits such as figs, prunes, and apricots can be presoaked or simmered in wine or fruit juice, then cooked on skewers.

You can also bake fruit on the hearth when you have a good hot fire going. Fill cored apples with raisins, brown sugar, and rum, wrap them in heavy-duty foil, and place them at the base of the fire to bake. Peeled bananas, brushed with lemon juice, rum, and melted butter, and sprinkled with brown sugar and spices, can be wrapped and cooked the same way. And children will love Banana Boats: Pull back an inch-wide strip of peel, slit the banana, and pack in chocolate chips and miniature marshmallows. Replace the peel, wrap the banana in foil, and place it near the fire to heat it through.

Or, if only "chestnuts roasting on an open fire" will do, just slash their shells with a sharp knife, grease them with vegetable oil, and place them in a corn popper (or wrap them in a sheet of heavy foil with holes punched in it); roast them 4 inches from the fire for 15 to 20 minutes.

THANKSGIVING DINNER

Shiitake Mushroom Soup

Honey-Glazed Turkey with Bourbon Gravy

Sausage Cornbread Stuffing

Parsnips and Peas in Tarragon Butter

Creamed Yams with Brown Sugar

Spicy Apple Chutney · Onion Marmalade

Honey-Pecan Ice Cream · Persimmon Cake

SERVES 12

▼

Thanksgiving brings out the traditionalist in almost everyone. Oyster, sausage, and chestnut stuffings all have their partisans, and the great cranberry sauce debate—whole-berry versus jellied—is sure to be revived. This holiday menu includes innovative touches that may even create some new traditions in your household. The turkey is roasted with bourbon, and unusual counterpoints are provided by an onion "marmalade" and a hot-and-sweet apple chutney.

One way to ensure everyone's comfort and satisfaction at Thankgiving dinner is to serve the meal buffet-style, but eat it as a sit-down dinner. Offering the food on a sideboard allows for extra space at the dining table, which your guests will appreciate while they enjoy the bounty of this harvest celebration.

The Thanksgiving dinner

Shiitake Mushroom Soup

More expensive—but also more deeply flavored—than button mushrooms, fresh shiitakes are now sold in the produce sections of many supermarkets.

1 stick (8 ounces) butter
1½ pounds fresh shiitake mushrooms,
    stems removed, caps sliced ¼-inch thick
2 cups chopped scallions
6 cloves garlic, minced

½ cup flour
8 cups canned chicken broth
½ teaspoon white pepper
1 tablespoon grated fresh ginger

1. In a medium saucepan, melt the butter over medium heat. Add the mushrooms, scallions, and garlic, and sauté until the mushrooms are well coated with butter, 5 to 8 minutes.

2. Stir in the flour and cook, stirring, until the flour is barely visible, 1 to 2 minutes. Stir in the broth and pepper, and bring the soup to a boil. Cover the pan, reduce the heat to medium-low, and simmer the soup until the mushrooms are very tender, about 20 minutes.

3. Just before serving, stir in the ginger.   *12 servings*

Honey-Glazed Turkey with Bourbon Gravy

To prepare this handsomely browned bird, you will need a roaster with a tight-fitting lid to seal in the bourbon-scented steam. When you add the whiskey, pour it directly into the bottom of the pan, rather than over the bird. The rich fumes will both flavor and self-baste the turkey as long as the moisture is sealed in, so be sure to leave the pan covered (don't peek even once) for the first 2½ hours of roasting.

12-pound turkey, rinsed
Sausage Cornbread Stuffing (recipe follows)
1 tablespoon salt
1 teaspoon pepper
½ cup honey

1 tablespoon soy sauce
2 cups bourbon
1 tablespoon butter
3 tablespoons flour

1. Preheat the oven to 350°.

2. Stuff the turkey loosely with the Sausage Cornbread Stuffing and truss it. Rub the outside of the turkey with the salt and pepper. Place the turkey, breast-side up, in a roasting pan.

3. In a small bowl, stir together the honey and soy sauce. Drizzle the honey mixture over the turkey to coat it completely. Pour the bourbon into the bottom of the roasting pan and cover the pan with a tight lid. Roast the turkey for 2½ hours without taking off the lid.

4. Baste the turkey with the pan juices, then roast it, uncovered, basting once or twice, for 20 to 30 minutes longer, or until an instant-reading meat thermometer inserted into the thickest part of the leg registers 170°. Should any portion of the turkey seem to be browning too quickly, cover it loosely with aluminum foil.

5. Transfer the turkey to a carving board and let rest for at least 15 minutes before carving.

6. Meanwhile, make the gravy: Pour the pan juices into a bowl; there should be about 3 cups. (If desired, place the bowl in the freezer until the fat congeals on top; skim off the fat before making the gravy.) In a small saucepan, combine the butter, ¼ cup of the pan juices, and the flour, and cook, stirring, over medium heat until the mixture is smooth and brown. Gradually add the remaining pan juices, whisking constantly until smooth.

7. Spoon the stuffing into a serving dish, carve the turkey, and serve with the gravy.

12 servings

In A Thousand Ways to Please a Family, a 1922 cookbook, a homemaker gave careful consideration to her Thanksgiving centerpiece. "I think an Indian basket filled with fruit would be the most appropriate thing—polished red apples and purple grapes. . . . Red and yellow corn would be charming, and these bright yellow squashes, and peppers. . . . And oak leaves, too. Of course we might hollow out pumpkins to hold the fruit and leaves, but I think I'd prefer the Indian baskets."

Sausage Cornbread Stuffing

This stuffing is best when prepared with homemade cornbread. Since there's always plenty to do on Thanksgiving day, you'll probably want to bake the bread in advance: it can be made a week ahead of time, wrapped, and frozen. If you don't have time to bake and are unable to buy cornbread, substitute six cups of packaged cornbread stuffing mix. Adjust the seasonings, if necessary.

Ceramic pots in realistic fruit and vegetable shapes are perfect for holding condiments and sauces on a Thanksgiving table. Real cabbages, winter squashes, or miniature pumpkins could also be hollowed out and used as serving dishes.

CORNBREAD
1½ cups flour
½ cup yellow cornmeal
⅓ cup (packed) dark brown sugar
2½ teaspoons baking powder
1 cup buttermilk, or 1 cup milk plus 1
    tablespoon vinegar
6 tablespoons butter, melted
1 egg, lightly beaten

STUFFING
½ pound spicy bulk sausage, crumbled
2 tablespoons butter

1 cup chopped leeks or onions
2 stalks celery, chopped (about 1 cup)
1 clove garlic, minced
1 small red bell pepper, chopped
    (about 1 cup)
¼ cup chopped parsley
1 teaspoon sage, crumbled
1 teaspoon thyme
1 teaspoon salt
½ teaspoon black pepper

1. Preheat the oven to 425°. Grease an 8-inch square baking pan.

2. Make the cornbread: In a large bowl, stir together the flour, cornmeal, sugar, and baking powder, and make a well in the center.

3. In a small bowl, stir together the buttermilk, melted butter, and egg. Pour the egg mixture into the dry ingredients and mix just until blended; do not overmix.

4. Spread the batter evenly in the prepared pan and bake for 25 to 30 minutes, or until a toothpick inserted in the center comes out clean and dry. Cool the bread in the pan on a rack for 10 minutes, then turn it out onto the rack to cool completely.

5. Preheat the oven to 250°. Cut the cooled cornbread into ¾-inch cubes and place them in a single layer on an ungreased baking sheet. Dry the cornbread in the oven for 1 hour, or until crisp; set aside.

6. Make the stuffing: In a large skillet, sauté the sausage over medium heat, breaking it up with a spoon, until the meat is no longer pink, 5 to 10 minutes.

7. Add the butter, leeks, celery, and garlic, and sauté until the leeks are softened but not browned, about 5 minutes. Increase the heat to medium-high, add the bell pepper, and sauté for 3 minutes.

8. Add the dried cornbread, parsley, sage, thyme, salt, and black pepper to the skillet, and mix well. Cool the stuffing slightly before using.   *Makes about 10 cups*

Parsnips and Peas in Tarragon Butter

Parsnips are sweeter when harvested after a frost; the cold converts some of their starch into sugar. In cold climates, they are sometimes left in the ground all winter and picked, at their sweetest, in the spring. Since fresh peas are not in season in November, you will probably have to use frozen peas (or canned baby peas) for this vegetable side dish. Should you find fresh peas, add them to the parsnips about 5 minutes earlier.

1½ cups canned chicken broth
1½ teaspoons tarragon
½ teaspoon white pepper
2 pounds parsnips, peeled and cut on the
  diagonal into ¼-inch-thick slices

2 packages (10 ounces each) frozen peas
1 stick (4 ounces) butter, cut into small
  pieces
2 tablespoons chopped parsley

1. In a medium saucepan, combine the broth, tarragon, and pepper, and bring to a boil over medium-high heat. Add the parsnips, cover, and simmer, turning frequently, until the parsnips are tender, 5 to 8 minutes.

2. Stir in the peas, cover, and cook for 3 minutes longer. Stir in the butter and parsley, and serve.

12 servings

Muffins or miniature breads baked in old-fashioned molds provide tasty, eye-catching additions to the Thanksgiving meal. Corn, cranberry, pumpkin, or apple muffins would all be fine accompaniments for this menu.

Creamed Yams with Brown Sugar

These rich mashed sweet potatoes are easy to prepare and delectable to eat. The yams can be boiled (or cooked in the microwave, if you prefer) the day before Thanksgiving. Wrap and refrigerate them overnight, but let them return to room temperature before you peel and mash them. Soften the butter slightly so that it can be stirred in easily along with the cream and sugar. Place the creamed potatoes in a casserole and reheat them in the oven while the turkey rests before carving.

6 pounds yams
¾ cup heavy cream

1 stick (4 ounces) butter
⅓ cup (packed) brown sugar

1. In a large pot of simmering salted water, cook the yams until tender, 30 to 35 minutes; drain. When they are just cool enough to handle, peel the yams and mash them until smooth.

2. Add the cream, butter, and sugar, and stir until well blended.

12 servings

Spicy Apple Chutney

This unusual condiment is an ideal complement to turkey, or any hot or cold meat or sharp cheese. The chutney can be made a few days in advance (the weekend before Thanksgiving might be a good time to cook it) and refrigerated in a covered jar.

6 Granny Smith or other tart, firm apples
  (about 3 pounds), peeled and sliced
    ½ inch thick
1 medium onion, coarsely chopped
1 small green bell pepper, finely chopped
½ cup fresh or frozen cranberries

2 cloves garlic, minced
2 cups white wine vinegar
1 cup (packed) brown sugar
2 tablespoons grated fresh ginger
1 tablespoon mustard seeds
¾ teaspoon salt

1. In a large saucepan, combine the apples, onion, bell pepper, cranberries, and garlic. Stir in the vinegar, sugar, ginger, mustard seeds, and salt, cover the pan, and bring to a boil over medium-high heat. Uncover the pan and cook until the apples are soft, 8 to 10 minutes.

2. Reduce the heat to medium-low and cook, uncovered, stirring occasionally, until the chutney is thick, about 1½ hours. *Makes about 6 cups*

Spicy Apple Chutney in the making

Onion Marmalade

The consistency, not the flavor, of this onion relish resembles that of marmalade—although the recipe does call for a bit of the orange preserve for sweetness.

*2 pounds Spanish onions, coarsely
    chopped (about 4 cups)*
6 cloves garlic, minced
⅓ cup olive oil
2 tablespoons orange marmalade

2 tablespoons white wine vinegar
1 tablespoon brown sugar
2 teaspoons chopped parsley
1 teaspoon salt
½ teaspoon pepper

    1. In a medium saucepan, combine the onions, garlic, and oil. Cover the pan and cook over medium heat, stirring occasionally, until the onions are golden brown and soft, about 20 minutes.

    2. Stir in the orange marmalade, vinegar, sugar, parsley, salt, and pepper, and transfer the mixture to a glass jar or bowl. Let the mixture cool to room temperature. If not serving immediately, cover and refrigerate it. Let the onion marmalade return to room temperature before serving.   *Makes about 2½ cups*

Honey-Pecan Ice Cream

This rich dessert can be frozen in any of the automatic home ice-cream makers available today. Of course, an old-fashioned hand-cranked wooden ice-cream freezer, filled with crushed ice and rock salt, will also do an excellent job.

3 cups heavy cream
2 cups milk
1 cup honey

6 egg yolks, lightly beaten
2 teaspoons vanilla extract
2 cups toasted pecans, coarsely chopped

    1. In a double boiler, combine the cream, milk, and honey. Cook the mixture over boiling water, stirring constantly, until the cream mixture is hot but not boiling, about 7 minutes.

    2. Gradually drizzle a few tablespoons of the hot cream mixture into the beaten egg yolks, stirring constantly, then whisk in about 1 cup more of the hot cream mixture. Whisk this egg mixture into the cream mixture remaining in the double boiler and cook over medium heat, stirring constantly, until the custard coats the back of a spoon, about 5 minutes.

    3. Remove the top of the double boiler from the heat and let the custard cool to room temperature. Stir in the vanilla. Chill the custard in the refrigerator for 1 hour.

    4. Pour the custard into the canister of an ice-cream maker and freeze according to the manufacturer's instructions. When the mixture is half-frozen, stir in the pecans and continue freezing. When the ice cream is fully frozen, cover the canister with plastic wrap and keep it in the freezer until ready to serve.   *Makes about 2 quarts*

According to Margaret E. Sangster's Good Manners for All Occasions, published in 1904, Thanksgiving is not only a joyous festival, but also a time to extend hospitality in its truest form: "Dear to every American heart is Thanksgiving. . . . Long may we keep this beautiful and happy day, not forgetting to invite to our dinner of turkey and accompaniments the stranger, the homeless, and the lonely."

Persimmon Cake

Persimmon desserts are an autumn specialty in the South and southern Midwest, where the native variety of this brilliant orange fruit grows wild. However, the persimmons most commonly found in American markets today are two cultivated Japanese types: the deep orange, plum-size Hachiya, and the smaller, paler Fuyu. For this cake, either variety of persimmons must be ripe to the point of bursting with juice. (Although the Fuyu variety is edible when hard, this recipe requires soft fruit that can be mashed to a pulp.) It would be wise to buy the persimmons early so that there's time to ripen them for a few days, if necessary, by placing them in a small plastic or paper bag with an apple or banana and leaving them at room temperature until they are completely soft. If you cannot find persimmons, you can make this spicy, plum-pudding-like cake with a cup of thick applesauce instead.

A resourceful hostess contributed this hint to the 1905 Good Housekeeping Discovery Book: "A plum pudding stuck to the mold and broke in half a dozen pieces. . . . I patched it together with white of egg brushed on each broken piece with a feather. Then I took the rest of the white, beat it quickly to a froth, added a spoonful of powdered sugar and a dash of vanilla. I spread it over the pudding . . . browned it slightly in a hot oven. . . . The compliments I had on my beautiful looking pudding made me smile."

1¼ cups flour	*1 cup (packed) brown sugar*
1 teaspoon baking powder	*½ cup heavy cream*
1 teaspoon baking soda	*2 eggs*
½ teaspoon cinnamon	*3 tablespoons dark molasses*
½ teaspoon ground ginger	*2 tablespoons butter, melted and cooled*
½ teaspoon nutmeg	*1 teaspoon vanilla extract*
¼ teaspoon salt	*1 cup raisins*
1 cup persimmon pulp (about ¾ pound)	

1. Preheat the oven to 350°. Butter and flour a 6-cup fluted (turk's-head or kugelhopf) mold.

2. In a small bowl, stir together the flour, baking powder, baking soda, cinnamon, ginger, nutmeg, and salt; set aside.

3. In a large bowl, combine the persimmon pulp, sugar, cream, eggs, molasses, butter, and vanilla, and stir until well blended.

4. Gradually add the dry ingredients, mixing until completely incorporated. Stir in the raisins.

5. Pour the batter into the prepared mold. Rap the mold once or twice on the counter to remove any air pockets. Bake for 1 hour, or until the cake shrinks from the sides of the pan and a toothpick inserted in the center of the cake comes out clean and dry.

6. Let the cake cool in the mold on a rack for 20 minutes, then turn the cake out onto the rack to cool completely.   *12 servings*

Persimmon Cake and Honey-Pecan Ice Cream

BRINGING IN THE SHEAVES

To give your Thanksgiving dinner an inviting country feeling, fashion some tabletop wheat sheaves that truly bring the harvest home. These diminutive bundles of grain can be used to add rustic charm to your home throughout the autumn.

Most craft and hobby shops stock wheat, as do some florists; if you live in a wheat-growing area, the materials may be yours for the asking. The two smaller sheaves shown here are made with a common bearded wheat; the taller sheaf is made of beardless wheat. Rye, barley, and oats could be substituted, as could wild grasses such as foxtails.

Wheat stalks are sold in lengths up to three or four feet, so it will be necessary to trim them. Cut the stalks above the first joint (a knob visible on the stalk) and slide off the sheaths, leaving clean, smooth shafts. Gather a good-size handful of the stalks into a bundle and bind them tightly with an elastic band. Put another, slightly looser, elastic band around the bundle. Then, neatly insert single stalks around the circumference of the bundle, keeping them side by side to create a smooth outer layer. Gripping the sheaf with one hand above and one below the elastic band, gently twist this outer layer. To finish the sheaves, use scissors to trim the bottoms of the stalks to a uniform length. Cover the elastic band with a strand of raffia (sold in craft shops) or with a ribbon. Strike the bottom of the sheaf on a flat surface to even the stalks; the sheaf should then be able to stand by itself on a tabletop.

Winter

*a time for warm
welcomes and merry
feasting*

The flame of true hospitality burns brightest against the snow and ice of the winter months. Remember the pure pleasure of coming in from the cold after skating or skiing. Then, imagine the joy of welcoming friends into a warm house, where you offer comfort and sustenance in the spirit of the season. This is the promise of winter entertaining.

When it's cold outside, the kitchen becomes a cozy retreat, a place where hours can be spent with the family while tending a simmering pot of stew or baking batch after batch of cookies. As the holidays approach, think about inviting friends over to share in these joyous occasions. Ring in the Yuletide by having loved ones, young and old, help to trim the tree; reward them with a generous buffet supper and plenty of gingerbread cookies. When New Year's Eve arrives, celebrate it with traditional glitter and gaiety. And observe Twelfth Night, on the fifth of January, with a special dinner to mark the end of the holiday season.

Tabletop flourishes of red, green, and gold enhance winter's cheery celebrations.

SKATING PARTY SUPPER

Lamb Stew with Winter Vegetables

Rice-Corn Bread

Thyme Butter

Mixed Green Salad

Apple Crumb Pie with Walnut Crust

SERVES 6

▼

A moonlight skating party would be a fanciful and romantic prelude to this meal, but an afternoon of any winter sport—cross-country skiing, hiking, or simply playing in the snow—calls for just such a hearty supper. Set the kitchen table with whimsical winter accessories, such as sparkling snow domes and snowflake candleholders, then gather your friends for a warming repast. The main dish is lamb stew, made with parsnips and winter squash and served with fresh, hot bread and herbed butter. A salad of watercress or other tart greens would help offset the richness of the stew.

Later, after games or conversation—or another quick trip outdoors to admire a starry winter sky—finish the meal with steaming mugs of coffee (spiked with applejack, if you like) and generous slices of apple pie.

Lamb Stew with Winter Vegetables

Although most vegetables, from asparagus to pumpkins, are available fresh, frozen, or canned all year round, it's very much in the country spirit to honor the traditional seasons of the garden. Acorn squash and parsnips, called for in this recipe, are typical "winter vegetables." In days gone by, they would have been stored in the root cellar, to furnish the table through the months when the garden was buried under snow. You can make this winter-worthy lamb stew in advance and reheat it at serving time; in fact, its flavor will improve if you do so. Don't be put off by the quantity of garlic called for; slow cooking mellows its flavor to a savory sweetness.

Your attic (or your child's toy chest) might yield charming accessories like the baby- and doll-sized caps, socks, and gloves that warm this winter table. If no such diminutive creations turn up, make a survey of local thrift shops—or knit your own.

¾ cup flour

1 teaspoon salt

½ teaspoon pepper

3 pounds stew lamb, cut into 2-inch chunks

4 tablespoons oil

6 medium parsnips, peeled and cut into
   1½-inch chunks (about 2 cups)

1¼ cups chopped leeks

15 cloves garlic, peeled

1 can (35 ounces) whole tomatoes, with
   their juice

2 teaspoons thyme

1 medium acorn squash, quartered,
   peeled and cut into ½-inch-thick slices

½ pound small mushrooms

2 tablespoons chopped parsley, for garnish

1. In a shallow bowl, combine the flour, salt, and pepper. Dredge the lamb in the seasoned flour, tapping off the excess; reserve the excess flour.

2. In a Dutch oven or flameproof casserole, heat 3 tablespoons of the oil over medium-high heat. Add the lamb to the pan and cook until the meat is evenly browned, about 8 minutes.

3. Stir in the reserved seasoned flour mixture, and cook, stirring, until the flour is absorbed. Add the parsnips, leeks, garlic, and remaining 1 tablespoon oil, reduce the heat to medium, and cook, stirring, for 10 minutes.

4. Stir in the tomatoes with their juice and the thyme, and bring the liquid to a boil over medium-high heat. Cover the pan, reduce the heat to medium-low, and simmer until the vegetables are slightly softened, about 20 minutes.

5. Add the acorn squash and mushrooms, and cover the pan. Cook, stirring occasionally, until the lamb is tender, another 40 minutes.

6. Ladle the stew into shallow soup bowls and serve hot, garnished with the parsley.   *6 servings*

Rice-Corn Bread

This bread is based on an old South Carolina recipe called "philpy," which was made with white rice and rice flour. Here, brown rice is combined with cornmeal for a more healthful bread with a slightly nutlike flavor.

2 cups white cornmeal
1½ teaspoons baking powder
1½ teaspoons baking soda
1 teaspoon salt

2 cups cooked brown rice
1½ cups buttermilk
2 eggs, lightly beaten
2 tablespoons butter, melted

1. Preheat the oven to 450°. Butter two 8 x 2-inch round cake pans.
2. In a medium bowl, blend the cornmeal, baking powder, baking soda, and salt; set aside.
3. In a large bowl, mash the rice with a wooden spoon. (Or, pulse it in a food processor for about 15 seconds.) Add the buttermilk, eggs, and butter.
4. Add the dry ingredients to the rice mixture and beat until well blended. Pour the batter into the prepared pans and spread it evenly with a rubber spatula. Rap the pans once or twice on the counter to remove any air pockets.
5. Bake for 30 minutes, or until the breads pull away from the sides of the pans and the tops are light golden. Serve hot. *Makes two 8-inch round loaves*

A dinner party is the perfect time to show off a collection of favorite objects, like the snow domes above. Or, revive the old dinner-party custom of giving favors: Set a small, inexpensive gift at each guest's place.

Thyme Butter

Easy to make, savory herbed butter is a wonderful complement to fresh, hot bread. You can substitute another herb, such as oregano, basil, or tarragon, if you prefer. Should there be any leftover thyme butter, it can be spread on toast or used to dress cooked green vegetables or potatoes.

1 stick (4 ounces) unsalted butter,
*   softened to room temperature*

2 tablespoons chopped fresh thyme, or
*   1 teaspoon dried*

1. In a small bowl, stir together the butter and thyme until well blended.
2. Cover the bowl and refrigerate for at least 3 hours, or up to 1 week (the flavor will intensify with time). The butter may also be frozen for up to 2 months.
3. Let the butter return to room temperature before serving. *Makes ½ cup*

Apple Crumb Pie with Walnut Crust

Although apples are available all year round, they are at their best soon after the harvest in the autumn and early winter. What better time to make this delicious dessert? Flavored with walnuts, this pie's crumbly topping is like the crust of an apple crisp. Serve the pie slightly warm, topped with whipped cream or vanilla ice cream.

PASTRY
⅔ cup finely chopped walnuts
1 cup flour
½ teaspoon salt
2 tablespoons dark brown sugar
3 tablespoons chilled butter, cut into pieces
2 tablespoons chilled vegetable shortening
3 to 4 tablespoons ice water

FILLING
3 tablespoons flour
3 tablespoons dark brown sugar
1 teaspoon cinnamon

1 cup light or dark raisins (optional)
3 large Granny Smith or other flavorful
    apples (about 1½ pounds)

TOPPING
½ cup flour
⅓ cup (packed) dark brown sugar
⅓ cup chilled butter
½ cup coarsely chopped walnuts
½ teaspoon cinnamon
½ cup heavy cream
1 tablespoon confectioners' sugar

1. Preheat the oven to 375°.

2. Make the pastry: Spread the walnuts in a shallow baking pan and toast them in the oven, stirring occasionally, for 10 to 12 minutes, or until golden brown; set aside to cool slightly. Turn off the oven.

3. In a large bowl, combine the cooled walnuts, the flour, salt, and brown sugar. With a pastry blender or two knives, cut in the butter and shortening until the mixture resembles coarse crumbs.

4. Sprinkle 2 tablespoons of the ice water over the mixture and toss it with a fork. The dough should be just barely moistened, enough so it will hold together when it is formed into a ball. If necessary, add up to 2 tablespoons more water, 1 tablespoon at a time. Form the dough into a flat disk, wrap in plastic wrap, and refrigerate for at least 30 minutes.

5. Meanwhile, make the filling: In a large bowl, stir together the flour, brown sugar, cinnamon, and raisins, if using; set aside.

6. Peel, core, and thinly slice the apples, then add them to the flour mixture and toss until well coated; set aside.

7. Preheat the oven to 375°.

8. On a lightly floured surface, roll the dough out to a 12-inch circle. Fit the dough into a 9-inch glass pie plate. Trim the overhang to an even ½ inch all the way around. Fold the overhang under and crimp the dough to form a decorative border. Prick the pastry with a fork.

9. Spoon the apple mixture into the pie shell, mounding it toward the center. Pat the filling down gently without compacting it.

A Thousand Ways to Please a Family, published in 1922, told of a January skating party, at which the hostess thoughtfully provided extra wraps for her friends: "I intend to see that my guests are comfortably dressed! We're coming back here for supper, you know, and I don't want my party spoiled by any frozen fingers or nipped noses."

10. Make the topping: In a small bowl, combine the flour and brown sugar. Using a pastry blender or two knives, cut in the butter until the mixture resembles coarse crumbs. Stir in the walnuts and cinnamon.

11. Sprinkle the topping over the filling, covering it completely, and bake for 45 to 55 minutes, or until the apples are tender and the topping begins to brown.

12. Just before serving, in a medium bowl, whip the cream with the confectioners' sugar until stiff. To serve, cut the pie into wedges and top each serving with a dollop of whipped cream.   *Makes one 9-inch pie*

Apple Crumb Pie with Walnut Crust

CHILLY-DAY DRINKS

On a frigid winter day, even the most devoted skiers, skaters, and snowman-builders look forward to coming indoors to sip a steaming cup of some delicious drink. And hearth-huggers whose only winter "sports" consist of shoveling the driveway will find these hot beverages especially appealing.

All these warming potions can be poured into a thermos and enjoyed outdoors, or quickly prepared upon returning from a foray into the cold. Two of the drinks include optional alcoholic ingredients; if you prefer their flavor minus most of their spirited effect, heat the beverage, uncovered, for a few minutes extra to allow some of the alcohol to cook off.

HOT GRAPE LEMONADE

In a medium saucepan, combine 3 cups white grape juice, 1 cup strained fresh lemon juice, and 2 tablespoons sugar. Cook over medium heat until hot. Garnish with lemon slices.

HOT FRUIT PUNCH

In a medium saucepan, combine 1½ cups strained fresh orange juice, ½ cup strained fresh lemon juice, 1 cup cranberry juice, 1 cup water, and ½ cup sugar. Cook over medium heat until hot. Garnish with orange slices.

MINT COCOA CUP

In a saucepan, scald 4 cups milk. In a small bowl, stir together 6 tablespoons unsweetened cocoa powder and ½ cup sugar. Gradually add 1 cup of the hot milk, stirring until smooth, then stir the cocoa mixture into the remaining milk in the pan and cook over low heat until hot. Add 2 tablespoons crème de menthe and cook for 1 minute longer. (A few drops peppermint extract per cup may be substituted for the crème de menthe.) Garnish with whipped cream or marshmallows.

MULLED COCOA

In a saucepan, scald 4 cups milk with ½ teaspoon cinnamon and ⅛ teaspoon nutmeg. In a heatproof bowl, stir together ½ cup unsweetened cocoa powder, 6 tablespoons sugar, and ¼ teaspoon salt. Gradually add 2 cups boiling water, stirring until smooth. Pour the cocoa mixture into the spiced milk, then add 1 teaspoon vanilla and cook over low heat, stirring constantly, for 2 minutes. Add ¼ cup brandy and cook for 1 minute longer.

Before you venture out into the cold, prepare a warming beverage to carry along. Clockwise from lower left: Hot Grape Lemonade, Hot Fruit Punch, Mint Cocoa Cup.

TREE TRIMMING
PARTY

Chicken-Vegetable Soup

Spinach and Bacon Salad with Garlic Croutons

Spicy Beef Pasties

Brandied Eggnog

Party Gingerbread Cookies

SERVES 6

▼

Kick off the Christmas season with a tree trimming party: Invite friends to help you hang your own ornaments or ask them to bring along homemade decorations such as popcorn balls or cranberry garlands. Your guests might also enjoy spending part of the evening creating their own ornaments or treats to take home: Set out tubes of colored icing, dried fruit, and candies to decorate gingerbread cookies, or provide materials and instruction books for making festive origami figures.

Whatever the plan, this type of casual buffet is an easy way to entertain during the hectic holiday period. Have bowls of oranges, apples, popcorn, and candy canes—seasonal symbols in themselves—available for nibbling throughout the evening. Serve the soup in mugs, and the pasties—beef-filled turnovers—on a platter, to be eaten with either forks or fingers. Everything can be prepared ahead of time, and each of the recipes in this menu can easily be doubled for a larger group.

Chicken-Vegetable Soup

Cauliflower, carrots, and kale are widely available in winter, but ripe tomatoes may be hard to find. Canned tomatoes (preferably Italian-style plum tomatoes) may be used instead. This chunky soup can be prepared, through Step 3, a few days ahead of time; add the chicken, parsley, and seasonings just before serving.

3 tablespoons vegetable oil

2 medium leeks, coarsely chopped (about 2 cups)

3 cloves garlic, minced

8 cups canned chicken broth

2 cups drained, coarsely chopped canned tomatoes, or 3 medium fresh tomatoes, seeded and chopped

2 cups cauliflower florets

2 medium carrots, diced (about 1¼ cups)

4 large kale leaves, shredded, or 3½ cups shredded cabbage

1 teaspoon marjoram or oregano

½ cup elbow macaroni or other small pasta

2 cups diced cooked chicken (about 10 ounces)

¼ cup chopped parsley

½ teaspoon pepper

Salt

1. In a stockpot or large saucepan, heat the oil over medium heat. Add the leeks and garlic, and sauté until translucent, about 5 minutes.

2. Add the chicken broth, tomatoes, cauliflower, carrots, kale, and marjoram, and bring to a boil. Reduce the heat to medium-low, cover, and simmer the soup for 10 minutes.

3. Increase the heat to medium-high. When the soup comes to a full boil, stir in the macaroni, and cook, uncovered, for 8 minutes.

4. Stir in the chicken, parsley, pepper, and salt to taste. When the soup returns to a boil, reduce the heat to medium and simmer the soup until the chicken is heated through, about 2 minutes longer. *6 servings*

Chicken-Vegetable Soup

Spinach and Bacon Salad with Garlic Croutons

Spinach—especially the curly-leaved type—must be washed carefully, or you risk getting bits of grit in your salad. The easiest method is to plunge the trimmed leaves into a sinkful of lukewarm water to which a little salt has been added. Swish the spinach around in the water, then leave it for a moment to let the sand settle to the bottom. Lift out the leaves, drain and rinse the sink, and repeat this process until no grit remains. To lighten your last-minute workload, wash the spinach a day in advance; shake it dry, roll it in paper towels, then place it in a plastic bag and refrigerate until needed.

GARLIC CROUTONS
Six ½-inch-thick slices firm whole-wheat bread
½ cup olive oil
¼ cup chopped parsley
2 cloves garlic, minced
½ teaspoon pepper

SALAD AND DRESSING
¼ pound bacon
½ pound fresh spinach

1 large tomato, cut into wedges
1 red onion, thinly sliced
⅔ cup olive oil
⅓ cup lemon juice
4 teaspoons Dijon mustard
½ teaspoon salt
½ teaspoon pepper
3 hard-cooked eggs, coarsely chopped

1. Preheat the oven to 375°. Line a baking sheet with foil.
2. Make the croutons: Cut the bread into cubes. In a medium bowl, stir together the olive oil, parsley, garlic, and pepper. Add the bread cubes and toss until well coated.
3. Spread the bread cubes in an even layer on the prepared baking sheet and bake for 15 to 20 minutes, or until golden.
4. Meanwhile, make the salad: In a medium skillet, cook the bacon over medium heat until crisp, about 10 minutes. Drain the bacon on paper towels; crumble and set aside.
5. Tear the spinach into bite-size pieces and place them in a large salad bowl.
6. Add the tomato and onion slices to the spinach; set aside.
7. Make the dressing: In a small bowl, whisk together the olive oil, lemon juice, mustard, salt, and pepper.
8. Just before serving, add the chopped eggs, crumbled bacon, and croutons to the salad. Pour the dressing over the salad and toss well. Serve immediately.

6 servings

In The Country Kitchen, Della Lutes recalled her mother's full-bodied vegetable soup, which you "had to chew a little. . . . This soup was the dinner. No Melba toast accompanied it, nor any . . . other supplementary starches . . . . It was served in a huge china tureen and ladled into soup plates of generous size. It was 'eaten' with a spoon, but whether from the side, tip, or whole spoon I do not remember. I only remember that it was . . . licking good!"

Spicy Beef Pasties

Pasties, popularized in this country by 19th-century immigrants from Cornwall, England, were the lunchtime fare of Cornish miners. Unlike the traditional meat pies, which are quite mild in flavor, these are spiced with lively Mexican seasonings— chilies, coriander, cumin, and oregano.

The author of the turn-of-the-century Entertainments For All Seasons was very much in favor of homemade ornaments. "Among the decorations ingenious, loving fingers can make . . . are popcorn balls, the gingerbread men of our grandmother's days, supplemented by gingerbread fairies . . . festive garlands of cranberries . . . sticks of candy tied together with ribbon."

PASTRY
2 cups flour
⅔ cup yellow cornmeal
¼ cup chopped fresh coriander
1½ teaspoons salt
6 tablespoons chilled butter, cut into pieces
6 tablespoons chilled vegetable shortening
8 to 10 tablespoons ice water

FILLING AND GLAZE
1 small potato
½ pound ground beef

1 medium carrot, diced
1 cup chopped scallions
3 cloves garlic, minced
1 can (4 ounces) diced mild green chilies, drained
¼ cup chopped fresh coriander
1½ teaspoons ground cumin
1 teaspoon oregano, crumbled
½ teaspoon salt
½ teaspoon pepper
1 egg, lightly beaten

1. Make the pastry: In a large bowl, stir together the flour, cornmeal, coriander, and salt. With a pastry blender or two knives, cut in the butter and shortening until the mixture resembles coarse crumbs.

2. Sprinkle 8 tablespoons of the ice water over the mixture and toss it with a fork. The dough should be moistened just enough so that it holds together when it is formed into a ball. If necessary, add up to 2 tablespoons more water. Form the dough into a flat disk, wrap in plastic wrap, and refrigerate for at least 30 minutes, or until well chilled.

3. Meanwhile, make the filling: Peel and quarter the potato, then thinly slice each quarter. In a large bowl, combine the potato, ground beef, carrot, scallions, garlic, and green chilies. Add the coriander, cumin, oregano, salt, and pepper, and mix gently until well combined.

4. Preheat the oven to 375°. Line a baking sheet with foil and lightly grease the foil.

5. On a lightly floured surface, roll out the dough to a ¼-inch thickness. Using a saucer or a paper template, cut out twelve 5-inch rounds. Reroll and cut any scraps.

6. Spoon about ¼ cup of filling onto one side of each pastry round, leaving a ½-inch border around the edge. Brush the edge of the pastry with water, then fold the pastry to cover the filling, forming semicircular turnovers. Seal the edges by pressing them with the tines of a fork.

7. Place the pasties on the prepared baking sheet. Prick the tops of the pasties with a fork, then brush them with the beaten egg. Bake for 30 to 35 minutes, or until the pasties are golden brown. Serve hot, or at room temperature.   *Makes 12 pasties*

Spicy Beef Pasties and Spinach and Bacon Salad with Garlic Croutons

Brandied Eggnog and Party Gingerbread Cookies

Brandied Eggnog

This traditional recipe can be made richer by replacing some of the half-and-half with heavy cream. For an even thicker eggnog, whip the cream lightly before adding it.

2 cups milk	*¾ cup sugar*
1 cinnamon stick	*2 cups half-and-half or light cream*
1 vanilla bean, split (optional)	*¾ cup rum*
3 whole cloves	*¾ cup brandy*
Pinch of mace	*1½ teaspoons vanilla extract*
6 egg yolks	*About 1 teaspoon nutmeg*

1. In a heavy saucepan, combine the milk, cinnamon stick, vanilla bean (if using), cloves, and mace. Place the pan over very low heat and cook for 5 minutes.

2. Meanwhile, in a medium bowl, whisk together the egg yolks and sugar until well blended.

3. Increase the heat under the saucepan to medium and bring the milk to a simmer. Very gradually add the hot milk to the egg-yolk mixture, whisking constantly, then return the mixture to the saucepan and cook, stirring constantly, until the mixture is thick enough to coat the back of a wooden spoon, 2 to 3 minutes. Do not let the mixture boil.

4. Strain the eggnog into a large bowl and set aside to cool to room temperature.

5. Stir in the half-and-half, rum, brandy, vanilla extract, and ½ teaspoon of the nutmeg. Cover the bowl and refrigerate the eggnog for at least 2 hours, or overnight. Just before serving, dust the top with additional nutmeg to taste.   *6 servings*

Party Gingerbread Cookies

Decorate these cookies lavishly with icing and bits of dried fruit, or colored sugar and candies. You can use a heavy-duty plastic food storage bag as a disposable decorating bag: fill it with icing, then snip a tiny hole in one corner and squeeze the icing out through the opening. Note that a fairly wide range is given for the amount of flour in this recipe: the humidity, as well as the type of flour, can cause variations in the consistency of the dough. For cookies that are crisp but not hard, add just enough flour to make the dough manageable; chilling it as directed will help, too. And try to use as little flour as possible when rolling and cutting the dough.

2⅓ to 3 cups flour
2 teaspoons ginger
1 teaspoon cinnamon
½ teaspoon salt
1 stick (4 ounces) butter, softened to
    room temperature
¾ cup (packed) dark brown sugar
¼ cup molasses
1 egg

DECORATION AND ICING
Dried fruit, cut into small pieces
Slivered almonds
Shredded coconut
1¼ cups confectioners' sugar
2 tablespoons water
¼ teaspoon vanilla extract

1. In a medium bowl, stir together 2⅓ cups of the flour, the ginger, cinnamon, and salt; set aside.

2. In a large bowl, cream the butter and brown sugar. Stir in the molasses, then add the egg. Gradually add the flour mixture, beating well after each addition. Beat in up to ⅔ cup more flour, if necessary, until the dough is no longer sticky.

3. Turn the dough out onto a lightly floured surface and knead it lightly until smooth, about 2 minutes. Form the dough into a ball, flatten it into a disk, wrap it in plastic wrap, and refrigerate it for at least 1 hour, or overnight.

4. Preheat the oven to 350°. Lightly grease a baking sheet.

5. On a lightly floured surface, using a lightly floured rolling pin, roll out the dough to a ¼-inch thickness and cut it with floured cookie cutters. Place the cookies on the prepared baking sheet, leaving 1 inch of space between them, and decorate with dried fruit, almonds, and coconut. Gather, reroll, and cut the scraps of dough.

6. If you plan to string the cookies on ribbons for hanging, use a skewer or ice pick to pierce small holes at the tops of the cookies. Bake the cookies for 15 to 17 minutes, or until crisp.

7. Let the cookies cool on the baking sheet for 2 to 3 minutes, then transfer them to a rack to cool completely. If the holes have closed up, repierce them while the cookies are still warm.

8. Meanwhile, prepare the icing: In a small bowl, combine the confectioners' sugar, water, and vanilla, and stir until thick and smooth; set aside.

9. Fill a decorating bag or tube with the icing and pipe it onto the cookies. Add details with more bits of the dried fruit, if desired.   *Makes 2 to 3 dozen cookies*

The 1912 book Fairs and Fetes, *which suggested themes for charity bazaars, proposed a preholiday Fair of the Christmas Shops. One booth would be The Bake-Shop, displaying "all sorts of Christmas cakes . . . with an edge of holly made of candied cherries . . . fancy cookies of all kinds, and especially gingerbread men made to represent Santa Claus, decorated in icing—tracery of features, buttons and bag of presents on his back."*

SPONGE-PAINTED COOKIES

A. It's easiest to divide the dough in half and work with one portion at a time. Keep the second portion refrigerated.

B. Use the paints as they come from the tubes, or mix the colors. Use a separate applicator for each color.

C. Dip a sponge into a contrasting paint color and blot it briefly. Dab the painted cookies lightly with the sponge.

These "cookie" tree ornaments are a welcome change in a season known for an excess of goodies: they are not meant to be eaten! The flour-and-salt dough is cut and baked just like regular cookie dough. Then the "cookies" are decorated with acrylic paints—first coated with a solid color, then sponged with a contrasting color in a technique similar to that employed by 19th-century potters to produce spongeware. After the ornaments are sealed with polyurethane (which should preserve them indefinitely), they are ready to be hung on the tree—or given as special keepsakes to friends. This recipe makes about three dozen ornaments.

MATERIALS

· 2 cups flour · ½ cup salt · ¾ cup water ·
· Acrylic craft paint, one 2-ounce bottle each in off-white, blue, red, green, mustard yellow (or colors of your choice) ·
· Small disposable foam paint applicators or flat artists' brushes ·
· Small natural sea sponges ·
· Clear high-gloss polyurethane · Wooden skewers or toothpicks ·
· Large upholstery needle ·
· Ribbon, yarn, or cord for hanging ·

◆

DIRECTIONS

1. Preheat the oven to 225°. Line two baking sheets with foil.

2. In a large bowl, stir together the flour and salt. Gradually add the water, stirring with a spoon at first, then kneading the dough with your hands as it becomes too stiff to stir.

3. Roll out the dough to a ¼-inch thickness and cut it with cookie cutters (Illustration A). Gather, reroll, and cut any scraps.

4. Place the cookies on the foil-lined baking sheets, leaving 1 inch of space between them. Using a skewer or toothpick, pierce a hole at the top of each cookie. Bake the cookies for 2 hours, or until firm and dry on top.

5. Transfer the cookies to a rack to cool. (If any of the holes have closed up, repierce them while the cookies are warm.)

6. Using a disposable foam paint applicator, paint both sides and the edges of each cookie with a coat of acrylic paint (Illustration B). Set aside to dry for at least 15 minutes, or until dry to the touch.

7. Dip a natural sponge lightly into a contrasting paint color, blot it, then dab the painted cookies with the sponge (Illustration C). Set the sponged ornaments aside to dry for at least 1 hour.

8. Working in a well-ventilated place, dip a clean brush into polyurethane and coat one side of each ornament with it. Clear the hole with a toothpick. Place the ornaments on waxed paper and let dry (follow manufacturer's directions for drying time), then coat the other side and the edges.

9. Using a large upholstery needle if necessary, thread a piece of ribbon, yarn, or cord through the hole in each ornament, and knot it securely.

NEW YEAR'S EVE DINNER

Nantucket Scallop Soup

Herbed Cornish Hens with

Brown Rice and Chestnut Stuffing

Green Beans in Shallot Butter

Lettuce and Cherry Tomato Salad · Dinner Rolls

Caramel Custards with Warm Apricot Compote

SERVES 4

▼

New Year's Eve is the quintessential occasion for an elegant dinner party. Instead of a big bash, plan an intimate gathering for four. Start off the evening with a glass of champagne and keep the bubbly flowing throughout the meal—it complements every course.

You'll probably want to serve this dinner late, so that you finish at midnight in time for a New Year's toast. The late dinner hour will allow you plenty of time during the day for leisurely preparation of the food and the special setting. What makes this holiday table unique is its golden glow: Choose flatware and china with brass, bronze, or gold accents, and use metallic-threaded linens. Complement these accessories with a centerpiece of gilded nuts, pine cones, and fruit; tie golden ribbons on the stems of the glasses; and spill handfuls of gold and silver stars across the table.

Nantucket Scallop Soup

This light yet creamy soup is made with bay scallops; if only the larger sea scallops are available at your market, cut them into quarters before cooking them.

2 cups bottled clam juice	½ pound bay scallops
2 cups milk, scalded	⅓ cup chopped carrot
2 cups peeled, diced red potatoes	½ teaspoon salt
1 cup chopped onion	¼ teaspoon white pepper
2 cloves garlic, minced	⅓ cup finely chopped scallions
1 bay leaf	

    1. In a medium saucepan, combine the clam juice, milk, potatoes, onion, garlic, and bay leaf, and bring to a simmer. Cover the pan and cook until the potatoes are tender, about 30 minutes.

    2. Pour the soup through a sieve set over a bowl. Remove and discard the bay leaf. Using a wooden spoon, press the cooked vegetables through the sieve. Return the soup to the pan.

    3. Bring the soup to a boil, then reduce the heat so the soup simmers. Add the scallops, carrot, salt, and pepper, and cook for 5 minutes longer. Ladle the soup into individual soup plates, sprinkle each serving with the chopped scallions, and serve.

4 servings

Herbed Cornish Hens with Brown Rice and Chestnut Stuffing

Choose smooth, glossy chestnuts that feel heavy in your hand. They can be prepared ahead of time, but be sure to peel them while they are still warm. The shells are quite difficult to remove once the chestnuts have cooled.

STUFFING	CORNISH HENS AND GRAVY
1 pound unshelled chestnuts (about 36)	2 large Cornish hens, rinsed
½ pound country-style bulk sausage	1 teaspoon salt
1 cup coarsely chopped onion	¼ cup chopped parsley
3 cups cooked brown rice (1 cup raw)	3 cloves garlic, minced
1 cup coarsely chopped celery	1 teaspoon sage, crumbled
2 tablespoons chopped parsley	½ teaspoon pepper
1 teaspoon sage, crumbled	1 medium onion, thinly sliced
1 teaspoon salt	½ cup canned chicken broth
¾ teaspoon pepper	1 tablespoon cornstarch
½ teaspoon thyme	

1. Make the stuffing: Using a sharp paring knife, cut an X in the flat side of each chestnut shell. Place the chestnuts in a medium saucepan and add cold water to cover. Bring the water to a boil and cook for 20 to 25 minutes. Drain the chestnuts in a colander and cool them briefly under cold running water. While the chestnuts are still warm, remove the shells and peel off the paperlike skin.

2. Set the chestnuts aside to cool slightly, then coarsely chop them.

3. If the sausage is in a casing, remove and discard the casing. Crumble the sausage into a large, heavy skillet. Add the onion and cook over medium-high heat for 5 minutes, stirring occasionally.

4. Add the chopped chestnuts, brown rice, celery, parsley, sage, salt, pepper, and thyme, and toss lightly with two forks until very well combined. There should be about 5 cups of stuffing.

5. Preheat the oven to 425°.

6. Prepare the Cornish hens: Sprinkle the cavity of each hen with ½ teaspoon of salt. Fill each hen with about 1 cup of stuffing. Place the remaining stuffing in a greased baking dish, cover with foil, and set aside.

7. Truss the hens and rub them with the parsley, garlic, sage, and pepper. Place the onion slices in the bottom of a large roasting pan. Place the hens on top of the onions.

8. Roast the hens for 20 minutes, then reduce the oven temperature to 350°. Place the dish of stuffing in the oven. Roast the hens and stuffing for 40 to 45 minutes. Baste the hens occasionally with the pan juices while cooking. The hens are done when an instant-reading meat thermometer inserted into the thickest part of the thigh registers 165° and the juices run clear when the same area is pierced with the tip of a knife.

9. Transfer the hens to a warm serving platter and cover with foil to keep warm.

10. For the gravy, transfer the pan juices and onions to a small saucepan. In a small bowl, stir together the broth and cornstarch, then add this mixture to the pan. Bring to a simmer over medium-high heat and cook, stirring, until thickened, 2 to 3 minutes.

11. To serve, remove the trussing strings from the hens. Cut the hens in half and pour the gravy over them. Serve the extra stuffing on the side. *4 servings*

Some stationery stores offer pretty, ready-made place cards. If you prefer to make your own, keep a supply of patterned papers, cards, and metallic or fabric trimmings on hand and you'll be able to create personal place cards for any occasion.

Green Beans in Shallot Butter

Sautéed shallots dress up these crisp-tender green beans. If you can find small, slender beans, cook them whole; halve or sliver the beans if they are large or thick. For a dash of extra color, add some yellow wax beans to this side dish.

1 pound green beans
2 tablespoons butter
2 tablespoons olive oil

½ cup chopped shallots (about 3 ounces)
½ teaspoon salt
½ teaspoon pepper

    1. Cut the green beans into 2-inch lengths.
    2. In a medium skillet, heat the butter and oil over medium heat. Add the shallots and sauté until light golden, about 5 minutes.
    3. Add the green beans, salt, and pepper, and sauté until the beans are crisp-tender, 3 to 5 minutes longer. Serve hot.

4 servings

This 1911 exaltation of a midnight supper could well have been written about a New Year's Eve party: "The most enjoyable of all meals is that which is served as the clock strikes twelve. There is a delightfully effervescent gaiety in the air, and a flavor to the food which is lacking at other times. Even bread and butter or crackers and cheese taste like ambrosia, while daintier food has a flavor surpassing that mythical delicacy."

Caramel Custards with Warm Apricot Compote

As in the classic recipe for *crème caramel,* a layer of sugar in the bottom of each dish turns into a luscious caramel sauce for these custards. When the desserts are unmolded, the sauce coats the custard. If you prefer to serve the custards without unmolding them, the caramel will be a sweet surprise at the bottom of each dish.

CARAMEL CUSTARDS
¼ cup (packed) light brown sugar
4 eggs
3 tablespoons maple syrup
1½ cups heavy cream
½ teaspoon vanilla extract

APRICOT COMPOTE
¼ pound dried apricots
1 cup cranberry juice
½ teaspoon grated lemon zest
½ cup fresh or frozen cranberries (optional)
1 tablespoon dark rum

    1. Make the custards: Place 1 tablespoon of the brown sugar in the bottom of each of 4 individual soufflé dishes or 6-ounce custard cups. Spread the sugar into a smooth, even layer; set aside.
    2. Preheat the oven to 350°.
    3. In a large bowl, beat the eggs until light. Stir in the maple syrup, cream, and vanilla, and continue beating until well blended. Divide the custard evenly among the prepared dishes. Set the dishes in a roasting pan placed on the middle rack of the oven. Pour hot water into the pan to reach halfway up the sides of the dishes.
    4. Bake the custards for 35 to 40 minutes, or until they are firm and the tip of a knife inserted into the center comes out clean.
    5. While the custards are baking, make the apricot compote: In a medium saucepan, combine the apricots, cranberry juice, and lemon zest. Bring to a boil, then

reduce the heat, cover the pan, and simmer until the apricots are very tender, about 20 minutes. If using cranberries, add them to the apricot mixture 5 minutes before it is done. Set the mixture aside, uncovered, to cool slightly.

6. Using a potato masher, mash the apricots in the cooking liquid, leaving the fruit somewhat chunky. Stir in the rum, cover the pan, and set aside.

7. When the custards are done, remove them from the hot water bath and wipe the soufflé dishes dry. Immediately unmold the custards by running the tip of a knife around the edge of each dish, then carefully inverting the dish onto a dessert plate. Spoon some apricot compote over each custard and serve warm.   *4 servings*

Caramel Custards with Warm Apricot Compote

THE GOLDEN TOUCH

A. Wear rubber gloves when applying the gold paint. Use mineral spirits for any necessary cleanup.

B. A pair of tweezers or needlenose pliers is useful for holding the items when dipping them.

C. If the gilded items slip through the boughs, secure them to the branches with fine wire.

A gold-painted basket filled with pine boughs and gilded natural objects—its handle wrapped with glossy ribbon tied in a generous bow—makes a lavish statement in an entranceway or on a dining table. This basket is filled with pine cones, Brazil nuts, almonds, walnuts, hazelnuts, pomegranates, artificial berries, and fabric leaves. Gilded seed pods, gourds, dried natural leaves, or artificial flowers would also work well. The basket and most of its contents can be stored away and brought out as an annual holiday tradition when the season commences. Only the greens will need to be replaced from year to year.

It is an easy task to transform the basket and accessories with a coat of gold paint. A splint basket in a simple shape offers a receptive surface to paint applied with a brush or a foam applicator. However, spray paint will be more effective in covering the intricate weaving of a wicker basket.

The pine cones, nuts, pomegranates, fabric leaves, and sprigs of artificial berries can be either dipped into or brushed with the paint. An old cake cooling rack, placed over newspaper to catch the drips, is a good surface on which to dry them; a piece of wire mesh or screening—or a sheet of waxed paper—would also serve the purpose.

MATERIALS

· Large unfinished basket · 1 quart gold paint ·
· Large and small pine cones ·
· Sprays of artificial berries · Unshelled nuts · Pomegranates ·
· Artificial ivy and leaves · Pine boughs or other evergreens ·
· Ribbon · Green tissue paper (optional) ·
· Small disposable foam paint applicators · Tweezers or pliers ·
· Cooling racks or waxed paper ·

◆

DIRECTIONS

1. Working in a well-ventilated area, cover the basket, inside and out, with gold paint (Illustration A). Set the basket aside to dry.

2. Using tweezers or pliers, dip the pine cones, berry sprays, and nuts into the gold paint (Illustration B). Set aside to dry on the cooling racks placed over newspaper, or on waxed paper.

3. Using a disposable foam paint applicator, paint the pomegranates, ivy, and other leaves; set aside to dry.

4. Twine the painted ivy around the edge of the basket. Place the pine boughs in the basket and arrange the pine cones, nuts, berries, and pomegranates on top of them (Illustration C). If the basket is very deep, fill the bottom with crumpled green tissue paper, then place the pine boughs on top of it.

5. Wrap the handle of the basket with the ribbon and tie a bow at the top.

TWELFTH NIGHT DINNER

Mulled Wine • Smoked Fish Canapés

Roast Pork Loin with Sage

Prunes and Apricots in Port Wine

Sautéed Bell Peppers with Tarragon

Potato Cakes with Scallion Sour Cream

Chocolate-Almond Torte

SERVES 6

▼

Twelfth Night, celebrated on January fifth (the eve of Epiphany), is a time for festive dinners and parties. In some countries, gifts are exchanged on this occasion rather than on Christmas, and the traditional King's Cake is shared: the finder of the lucky bean baked into the cake is crowned King (or Queen). However you mark it, Twelfth Night provides a happy note on which to bring the holiday season to a close.

A suitable starter for this winter night's gathering is mulled red wine, accompanied with an appetizer of your choice. Smoked salmon with herbed cream cheese and cocktail breads is one luxurious and delectable possibility. Set a regal table, with touches of scarlet and gold and, if possible, a kingly crown. Conclude the meal with a luscious version of King's Cake: a dense chocolate-almond torte, topped with a glossy chocolate glaze.

Mulled Wine

Combining the wine with the fruit and spices a day in advance ensures that it will become thoroughly infused with their flavors. To retain as much as possible of the wine's alcohol content, keep the pot covered from start to finish. If you uncover it, especially while heating the wine, the alcohol will quickly begin to evaporate.

4 small apples
24 whole cloves
Two bottles (750 ml each) burgundy or
*   other full-bodied red wine*
4 medium oranges, sliced

2 cups orange juice
4-inch piece fresh ginger, thinly sliced
4 small cinnamon sticks
⅔ cup sugar

1. Stud each apple with 6 cloves. Place the apples in a large nonreactive pot and add one bottle of the wine, the orange slices, orange juice, ginger, and cinnamon sticks. Cover the pot and let stand at room temperature for at least 12 hours.

2. At serving time, add the second bottle of wine and the sugar, and stir well. Bring the mixture to a boil over high heat, then immediately remove the pot from the heat. Strain the mulled wine into a heatproof pitcher or punch bowl, and serve.

Makes about 12 cups

Roast Pork Loin with Sage

Buy a rolled and tied boneless pork loin for this recipe; it's easy to carve and there is no waste. Be careful not to overcook the pork, as this cut is quite lean; the meat should reach an internal temperature of no higher than 170°.

2 tablespoons olive oil
6 cloves garlic, minced
¼ cup chopped fresh coriander
1 tablespoon sage, crumbled

1 teaspoon salt
1 teaspoon pepper
4-pound center-cut boneless
*   pork loin*

1. Preheat the oven to 450°.

2. In a small bowl, combine 1 tablespoon of the oil, the garlic, coriander, sage, salt, and pepper, and mash the mixture to a paste.

3. Rub the remaining 1 tablespoon oil all over the pork loin, then rub the garlic mixture over the surface of the meat. Place the pork loin in a shallow roasting pan and pour in ½ cup of water. Place the pork loin in the oven and roast it for 20 to 25 minutes, basting several times.

4. Reduce the oven temperature to 325° and roast the pork for 1 hour to 1 hour and 10 minutes, or until an instant-reading meat thermometer registers 165° to 170°.

5. Let the pork stand at room temperature for 5 minutes before carving.

6 servings

*T*his advice, from the 1909 Handbook of Hospitality for Town and Country, *is, if anything, truer than ever today. "Our hostess will be wise if she does not attempt to do too many things on the day when she expects guests to dinner. . . . In order to make a dinner a delightful occasion, the lady of the house must be at her best, fresh and in good spirits. . . . It is better to have fewer persons present or fewer courses than to lose one's astral calm."*

The Twelfth Night dinner

Prunes and Apricots in Port Wine

This dried-fruit compote not only provides the perfect accompaniment to roast pork, but it can also be served as a dessert at another meal. You might like to offer the remaining port as an after-dinner drink. Its sweet, mellow flavor is certain to be welcomed on a chilly winter's night.

1 pound dried apricots
1 pound pitted prunes

2 cups port wine
2 tablespoons grated lemon zest

1. In a medium nonreactive saucepan, combine the apricots, prunes, port, and lemon zest, and bring to a boil over medium heat.

2. Reduce the heat to low, cover the pan, and simmer until the fruit is tender, about 15 minutes. If not serving immediately, transfer the fruit and liquid to a bowl, cover, and refrigerate.

Makes about 6 cups

Sautéed Bell Peppers with Tarragon

Red and yellow bell peppers are now available all year round in many supermarkets. Some stores offer orange, purple, and chocolate-brown peppers, as well.

3 tablespoons olive oil
2 red onions, thinly sliced
6 cloves garlic, minced
2 large green bell peppers, thinly sliced
2 large red bell peppers, thinly sliced

2 large yellow bell peppers, thinly sliced
2 teaspoons tarragon
¾ teaspoon salt
½ teaspoon black pepper
½ cup canned chicken broth

1. In a large skillet, heat the oil over medium heat. Add the onions and garlic, and sauté until light golden, about 5 minutes.

2. Add the bell peppers, tarragon, salt, and black pepper, and sauté until the peppers are coated with oil, 2 to 3 minutes longer.

3. Add the chicken broth, cover the pan, and cook until the peppers are limp, 1 to 2 minutes longer.

6 servings

A "jeweled" crown can be purchased at a costume or novelty shop, or, with a little ingenuity, made at home from foil, a scrap of velvet, and some old costume jewelry. The embroidered "royal" emblems—which can be attached to ribbons to serve as napkin rings—come from a notions counter.

Potato Cakes with Scallion Sour Cream

These lacy potato pancakes are topped with a savory sour cream. Do not grate the potatoes too far in advance, as they will begin to darken if left standing too long.

SCALLION SOUR CREAM
½ cup sour cream
½ cup finely chopped scallions
¼ teaspoon pepper

POTATO CAKES
2 pounds all-purpose potatoes

2 eggs, lightly beaten
¼ cup flour
2 cloves garlic, minced
½ teaspoon salt
½ teaspoon pepper
2 to 3 tablespoons olive oil

1. Make the scallion sour cream: In a small bowl, combine the sour cream, scallions, and pepper, and stir until blended. Cover and refrigerate until needed.

2. Peel the potatoes, then grate them on the coarse side of a grater into a large bowl. Add the eggs, flour, garlic, salt, and pepper, and stir until well blended.

3. Heat 1 teaspoon of the oil in a large, heavy nonstick skillet over medium heat. Drop ¼-cup portions of the potato mixture into the skillet and flatten each portion into a cake. Cook the potato cakes until the edges are crisp and browned, 3 to 4 minutes, then turn them and cook until golden brown, 3 to 4 minutes longer. Transfer the cooked potato cakes to a warm platter and cover them with foil to keep warm. Cook the remaining potato mixture in the same fashion, adding more oil as necessary to prevent sticking.

4. Serve the potato cakes with the scallion sour cream.

6 servings

Chocolate-Almond Torte

This nontraditional King's Cake (it's usually a ring of brioche) plays a pivotal role in the holiday celebration: A dried bean is baked into it, and when the cake is cut, the person who receives the slice containing the bean rules the day. Just a word of caution: Be sure to warn your guests about the bean before they take a bite of cake!

1 cup blanched whole almonds (about 4½ ounces)
1½ cups confectioners' sugar
3 whole eggs plus 1 egg white
⅔ cup flour
⅓ cup unsweetened cocoa powder
½ teaspoon baking powder

1½ sticks (6 ounces) butter, softened to room temperature
½ teaspoon almond extract
1 dried white bean, such as Great Northern
2 ounces semisweet chocolate, cut into pieces
¼ cup heavy cream
Candied violets, for garnish (optional)

1. Preheat the oven to 350°. Butter an 8 x 2-inch round cake pan, line the bottom with buttered waxed paper, and then flour the pan.

2. Place the almonds in a food processor and process, pulsing the machine on and off, for 5 to 10 seconds, or just until the almonds are finely ground. Do not overprocess or the nuts will turn into an oily paste.

3. Add the sugar and egg white, and pulse just until combined; set aside.

4. In a small bowl, stir together the flour, cocoa, and baking powder.

5. In a large bowl, combine the almond mixture with the butter and beat until creamy and light. Add the whole eggs, one at a time, beating well after each addition, then beat in the almond extract.

6. Gradually add the dry ingredients, beating just until combined; do not overbeat. Drop the bean into the batter and stir gently.

7. Spread the batter evenly in the prepared pan. Rap the pan once or twice on the counter to remove any air pockets. Bake for 30 to 35 minutes, or until the cake shrinks from the sides of the pan and a toothpick inserted in the center of the cake comes out clean and dry.

8. Let the cake cool in the pan on a rack for 15 minutes, then turn it out onto the rack to cool completely.

9. When the cake is cool, make the chocolate glaze: Place the chocolate and cream in a double boiler and heat over simmering water, stirring often, until the chocolate has melted and the mixture is smooth.

10. Remove the waxed paper from the cake, leaving the cake on the rack. Place a large sheet of waxed paper under the rack.

11. Pour the glaze onto the center of the cake and tilt the rack to allow the glaze to coat the entire top and sides (to keep the glaze smooth, do not attempt to spread it). Leave the cake on the rack until the glaze has set, or refrigerate it for a few minutes to set the glaze more quickly. When the glaze is firmly set, transfer the cake to a serving plate. Decorate the cake with candied violets, if desired. *Makes one 8-inch cake*

This single-layer almond-chocolate torte, enrobed in a chocolate glaze, is adorned with crystallized violets. If you prefer to decorate the cake with a lacy white pattern instead, place a doily on top and dust sifted confectioners' sugar over it, then carefully remove the doily.

Victorian Table Silver

Silver tableware, once found only in the homes of those "born with silver spoons in their mouths," began to make its appearance on middle-class American tables by the latter half of the 19th century. Its wider availability was the result of several factors: the discovery of Nevada's Comstock Silver Lode, which lowered the cost of silver ore; the invention of electroplating; and the beginning of mass production of silverware. There was a ready market for these newly available wares, as a fast-rising middle class strove to emulate the extravagant lifestyle of the upper class.

In the late 19th century, books such as *Waiting at Table, A Practical Guide*, by Mrs. John Sherwood, provided the upwardly mobile hostess with precise information on how to give a proper dinner party. The author noted that "The appointments of the modern dinner-table strikingly indicate that growth of luxury of which the immediate past has been so fruitful." Mrs. Sherwood's table-setting instructions are typical of the time: At each place, lay "two large dinner-knives and a small silver fish-knife, two large dinner-forks and a small silver fish-fork [and] a tablespoon for soup." On the sideboard, arrange "a row of large forks, a row of large knives, a row of small forks and small knives, a row of tablespoons, a row of ladles for the different sauce-boats, a row of dessert-spoons . . . the soup ladles, the fish slice and fork, and the carving knives and forks." Set each dessert plate with "a gold ice spoon, and a silver dessert knife and fork, or gold, as the case may be."

Descriptive details such as these merely hint at the dizzying variety of table silver available at the time. Manufacturers rose to the challenge of supplying implements to suit every occasion and every food, from the mundane to the exotic. A celebratory menu of the 1880s might have consisted of fifteen courses—from oysters to ices—followed by liqueurs, fruit, bonbons, demitasse, and brandy. In the era that inspired the term "conspicuous consumption," what more appropriate way to attack such a feast than with a unique utensil for each delicate morsel?

At right, treasures from a well-appointed Victorian table. **1.** Grape shears **2.** Ice spoon **3.** Nut dish/placecard holder **4.** Sardine fork **5.** Ice cream serving set **6.** Nut spoon **7.** Olive spoon/spear **8.** Sardine fork **9.** Bonbon scoop **10.** Fruit knife **11.** Individual sugar dish **12.** Strawberry fork **13.** Sugar spoon **14.** Fish serving set **15.** Bonbon scoops **16.** Pickle fork **17.** Jelly-roll knife or trowel **18.** Berry spoon **19.** Butter pick **20.** Jelly knife

Spring

*a time of renewal
and lighthearted
celebration*

S pring reveals a world reawakening. After the frosty
stillness of winter, shoots and buds burst forth, bringing with them the promise of new color in the garden
and new flavors on the table. The holidays and other
festive occasions that brighten spring's calendar offer ample opportunities to sample the sweetest "first fruits."

The period that begins with Mardi Gras culminates with
Easter: celebrate the former with a jazzy New Orleans-style buffet
supper, and the latter with a homey, relaxed Sunday brunch. The
silliness of April Fools' Day provides an amusing excuse for a
dinner party with a jocular theme, while high-school and college
graduations in May and June find thousands of students eager to
rejoice in their achievements by feasting with family and friends.
Spring is also the time to bring fresh flowers to the table, and to
savor the delicately tender salad greens and first-of-the-season
vegetables that act as a "spring tonic" for the taste buds.

The spirit of spring is expressed in table decorations from tulips to Easter eggs.

MARDI GRAS
SUPPER

New Orleans Milk Punch

Spicy Cajun Pecans • Creole Praline Almonds

Bouillabaisse Louisianne

Hot Herbed Croutons

Chicory and Cherry Tomato Salad

Sweet Potato Praline Tart

S E R V E S 8

▼

A time of unbridled merrymaking, Mardi Gras—Fat Tuesday—represents a final fling before the restrictions of Lent. To most Americans, the holiday is inseparably associated with New Orleans. The foods of this fascinating city—whether sophisticated Creole or down-home Cajun— have enjoyed great popularity in recent years. Even if you live outside the South, holding a Mardi Gras bash is a great way to enjoy some classic New Orleans dishes.

To help create the mood, fill the room with plenty of color, sparkle, and sound. Decorate the table with the masks, beads, sequins, feathers, and shiny "doubloons" that are associated with this event. Invite your friends to come to the party in costume or provide them with glittery masks as they arrive. And play some New Orleans-style jazz all evening long to keep the good times rolling.

New Orleans Milk Punch

Though somewhat similar to eggnog in flavor, this punch is not as rich. It can be served with dessert, or as a welcoming drink as guests arrive.

2 pints light cream or half-and-half
2 cups bourbon
1 teaspoon vanilla extract

3 tablespoons confectioners' sugar
½ cup heavy cream
½ teaspoon nutmeg

1. In a pitcher, stir together the light cream, bourbon, and vanilla. Add the sugar and stir until dissolved. Cover and refrigerate until well chilled.
2. In a small bowl, whip the heavy cream until stiff peaks form.
3. Stir the punch well, then pour it into small glasses or punch cups. Top each serving with a dollop of whipped cream and a sprinkling of nutmeg.   *8 servings*

The recipe for Almond Pralines in the turn-of-the-century Picayune's Creole Cook Book is accompanied by a description of a praline vendor in the New Orleans court district. "She made these ancient Creole 'Amandes Pralinées' a specialty, and served each almond separately, in a little cornet of paper, just as the ancient Creole dames do when serving them at their elegant festivities."

Spicy Cajun Pecans

These crunchy spice-coated nuts can be prepared up to three weeks in advance. Cool them completely before storing them in an airtight container.

1 egg white
2 tablespoons honey
1 tablespoon Worcestershire sauce
1 tablespoon butter, melted
1 teaspoon dry mustard
1½ teaspoons paprika

1 teaspoon salt
½ teaspoon black pepper
Pinch of cayenne pepper
8 ounces pecan halves
1 tablespoon sugar

1. Preheat the oven to 350°. Line a baking sheet with foil and grease lightly.
2. In a shallow bowl, combine the egg white, honey, Worcestershire sauce, butter, mustard, ½ teaspoon of the paprika, ½ teaspoon of the salt, ¼ teaspoon of the black pepper, and the cayenne, and stir until well blended; set aside.
3. In a medium saucepan of boiling water, blanch the pecans for 1 minute. Drain and immediately dredge them in the egg-white mixture.
4. With a slotted spoon, spread the nuts on the baking sheet, separating them if they clump together. Bake the nuts for 15 minutes.
5. Reduce the oven temperature to 325°, stir the pecans, and bake, stirring occasionally, for 15 to 20 minutes more, or until the nuts are crisp and dark brown.
6. Meanwhile, in a shallow bowl; combine the sugar with the remaining 1 teaspoon paprika, ½ teaspoon salt, and ¼ teaspoon black pepper. Dredge the nuts in the sugar-spice mixture while they are still hot, then set aside to cool.
Makes about 3 cups

Creole Praline Almonds

Although most people associate the word "praline" with the popular Southern pecan candy, it can also refer to other sugared nut delicacies, such as these glazed almonds.

½ cup sugar   *8 ounces whole almonds*

1. Preheat the oven to 425°. Line a baking sheet with foil and grease lightly.
2. Place the sugar in a shallow bowl.
3. In a medium-size saucepan of boiling water, blanch the almonds for 1 minute. Drain the almonds and immediately (while still steaming hot) dredge them in the sugar, turning them until the nuts are completely coated with liquified sugar.
4. With a slotted spoon, spread the almonds on the baking sheet, separating them if they clump together. Bake the nuts, stirring occasionally to ensure even browning, for 15 to 20 minutes, or until the sugar glaze is glossy and amber colored.

Makes about 1½ cups

New Orleans Milk Punch, Spicy Cajun Pecans, and Creole Praline Almonds

Bouillabaisse Louisianne

In France, the seafood stew called bouillabaisse is traditionally prepared with the best of the day's catch, flavored with typical Mediterranean ingredients such as olive oil, garlic, and tomatoes. Strictly speaking, a true French bouillabaisse cannot be made with North American seafood, but you can preserve the spirit of the dish by choosing whatever is freshest and best in your local market. This Louisiana version includes red snapper, oysters, shrimp, and crab. The soup base begins with a roux. One of the essential elements of Creole cooking, it is simply a blend of flour and fat, slowly cooked and stirred until it reaches the desired color—anywhere from pale blond to mahogany brown. For this recipe, the roux should be a rich caramel color.

Purple, green, and gold are the colors of Mardi Gras, and they appear on everything from food to the commemorative "doubloons" shown on page 93. Strands of beads or shimmery trimmings can be formed into napkin rings.

4 tablespoons butter
¼ cup olive oil
⅓ cup flour
3 carrots, diced (about 1⅓ cups)
2 stalks celery, diced (about 1 cup)
¼ pound shallots, minced
¾ cup chopped scallions
5 cloves garlic, minced
12 shucked oysters, liquid reserved
  and strained
4 cups canned chicken broth
1 can (14 ounces) whole tomatoes, juice
  strained and reserved

1 cup white wine
2 bay leaves
1½ teaspoons thyme
⅛ teaspoon cayenne pepper
1 pound red snapper fillet, cut into
  1½-inch squares
1 pound large shrimp, shelled and
  deveined
½ pound lump crabmeat
⅓ cup chopped parsley

1. Make the roux: In a large, heavy saucepan or soup pot, melt the butter over medium-high heat. Reduce the heat to low and stir in the olive oil, then gradually add the flour, stirring constantly, until the mixture is smooth and golden, about 5 minutes. Cook the roux, stirring constantly, until it is caramel colored, about 25 minutes longer.

2. Add the carrots, celery, shallots, scallions, and garlic, and cook, stirring frequently, until the vegetables just begin to brown, about 8 minutes.

3. Add the strained oyster liquid, the chicken broth, the tomatoes and their strained juice, the wine, bay leaves, thyme, and cayenne, and increase the heat to medium-high. Stir the mixture, breaking up the tomatoes with a spoon. When the liquid comes to a boil, reduce the heat, cover, and simmer for 20 minutes.

4. Add the snapper, shrimp, and oysters, and cook for 6 minutes longer. Add the crabmeat and parsley, and cook for 2 minutes. Remove and discard the bay leaves.

5. Ladle the soup into shallow soup plates.   *8 servings*

Hot Herbed Croutons

Unlike the usual croutons, which are small cubes of browned bread, these are generous slices of herbed toast, topped with Parmesan cheese. They are served alongside, rather than in, the soup. The herbed butter can be made in advance.

1 stick (4 ounces) butter, softened to
    room temperature
3 tablespoons chopped parsley
2 cloves garlic, minced
1 teaspoon sage, crumbled

1 teaspoon thyme
¼ teaspoon pepper
1 long loaf French bread (about 1 pound)
¼ cup grated Parmesan cheese

1. Preheat the broiler.
2. In a small bowl, cream the butter, parsley, garlic, sage, thyme, and pepper until smooth.
3. Cut the loaf of bread in half lengthwise and spread the cut sides with the herb butter. Sprinkle each half with 2 tablespoons of the Parmesan.
4. Place the bread, cut-side up, on a broiler pan and broil it 4 inches from the heat for 2 to 3 minutes, or until golden brown.
5. Cut each piece of bread crosswise into 12 thick slices.   *Makes 12 croutons*

Mardi Gras favors and decorations should be gaudy and playful. Buy fancy masks at a local costume shop or decorate plain masks with sequins, ribbons, feathers, or paint. Glittering trinkets, like these bead and "pearl" necklaces, are thrown from floats during the Mardi Gras parade.

Chicory and Cherry Tomato Salad

Chicory, sometimes called curly endive, has narrow leaves that curl into a frizz at the tips. The thick, tender leaves of Belgian endive come tightly furled into a tapered head. Both greens are slightly bitter and go well with a mild, creamy dressing. Edible flowers, such as red, orange, and yellow nasturtiums, can be added to the salad for a festive touch of color.

DRESSING
½ cup mayonnaise
½ cup sour cream
¼ cup chopped fresh dill, or 1 tablespoon dried
3 tablespoons lemon juice
½ teaspoon white pepper

SALAD
1 medium cucumber
1 medium head chicory
1 small Belgian endive
1 pint cherry tomatoes, halved
Edible flowers, for garnish (optional)

1. Make the dressing: In a small bowl, whisk together the mayonnaise, sour cream, dill, lemon juice, and pepper; set aside.
2. Make the salad: Score the cucumber skin with a fork. Cut the cucumber in half lengthwise, then cut it crosswise into ¼-inch-thick slices.
3. Tear the chicory and Belgian endive into bite-size pieces and place them in a large salad bowl. Add the cherry tomatoes and cucumber slices, and pour on the dressing. Toss gently. Garnish the salad with flowers, if desired.   *8 servings*

Sweet Potato Praline Tart

This luscious tart has a rich, creamy sweet potato filling, studded and topped with crisp bits of brittle pecan praline. Like many confectionery processes, making this kind of praline is somewhat tricky. Be sure to use a candy thermometer and follow the directions carefully so that the sugar syrup does not burn.

PRALINE
⅓ cup coarsely chopped pecans
½ cup granulated sugar
3 tablespoons water

PASTRY
1¼ cups flour
3 tablespoons granulated sugar
¾ teaspoon salt
6 tablespoons chilled butter, cut into pieces
1 egg yolk
1 to 3 tablespoons ice water

FILLING
2 tablespoons butter, softened to room
temperature

½ cup granulated sugar
2 tablespoons (packed) light brown sugar
2 sweet potatoes, baked, peeled, and
smoothly mashed (about 1¼ cups)
1 egg, lightly beaten
½ cup light cream or half-and-half
½ teaspoon vanilla extract
½ teaspoon allspice
¼ teaspoon cinnamon
¼ teaspoon ground ginger
¼ teaspoon salt
½ cup pecan halves

1. Make the praline: Preheat the oven to 350°. Line a 15½ x 10½-inch jelly-roll pan or baking sheet with foil and grease lightly. (If using a baking sheet, turn up the edges of the foil to form sides.)

2. Spread the chopped pecans in a small, shallow baking pan and toast them in the oven, stirring occasionally, for 5 to 7 minutes, or until golden brown. Set aside to cool slightly. Turn off the oven.

3. In a heavy saucepan, combine the granulated sugar and the water. Cook over medium heat, stirring constantly, until the sugar dissolves, about 3 minutes.

4. As soon as the sugar is dissolved, stop stirring the mixture. Place a candy thermometer (previously warmed in hot water) in the pan and bring the syrup to a boil over high heat. Boil the syrup until it is a caramel color and registers 340° on the candy thermometer, about 6 minutes. Remove the pan from the heat.

5. Add the toasted pecans and stir gently until they are thoroughly coated. Immediately pour the praline mixture into the foil-lined pan and spread it into a thin, even layer with a metal spatula. Set the praline aside until completely cool, then turn it out of the pan and peel off the foil. Finely chop the praline; set aside.

6. Make the pastry: In a large bowl, combine the flour, granulated sugar, and salt. With a pastry blender or two knives, cut in the chilled butter until the mixture resembles coarse crumbs.

7. In a small bowl, stir together the egg yolk and 1 tablespoon of the ice water. Sprinkle the egg-yolk mixture over the flour mixture and toss it with a fork. The dough

Sweet Potato Praline Tart

should be just barely moistened, enough so it will hold together when it is formed into a ball. If necessary, add up to 2 tablespoons more water, 1 tablespoon at a time. Form the dough into a flat disk, wrap in plastic wrap, and refrigerate for at least 30 minutes.

8. On a lightly floured surface, roll out the dough to a 12-inch circle. Fit the dough into a 9-inch tart pan. Trim off the overhang. Prick the bottom and sides of the pastry with a fork. Place the tart shell in the freezer to chill for at least 15 minutes before baking.

9. Preheat the oven to 375°.

10. Make the filling: In a large bowl, cream the butter, granulated sugar, and brown sugar until light and fluffy. Beat in the sweet potatoes until completely incorporated, then beat in the egg. Add the light cream, vanilla, allspice, cinnamon, ginger, and salt, and continue beating until the mixture is smooth. Stir in the pecan halves and ½ cup of the chopped praline.

11. Spread the filling evenly in the tart shell, then sprinkle the remaining praline over the filling. Bake the tart for 35 to 40 minutes, or until the crust is golden.

Makes one 9-inch tart

INTRIGUING INVITATIONS

The party starts early when you send out handsome handmade invitations to your gathering, whether casual or formal. Note cards, paper, and envelopes in a rainbow of hues can be found at many stationery stores, along with an equally wide range of pens, inks, markers, and colored pencils.

Decorate your invitations with ribbons, stickers, appliqués, or flat metal cutouts. Glue pressed flowers to garden-party cards, or adorn holiday invitations with pictures clipped from Christmas cards you've saved. Keep in mind that rubber stamps can be made from any printed image, while stamps in simple shapes can be cut from art-gum erasers. Any color scheme is possible if you use felt-tipped pens to ink the stamps. It's also fun to use fruits

and vegetables as stamps: Dip half a chili pepper, radish, or lemon into acrylic paint, then press it gently onto the paper.

Give as much thought to wording an invitation as you do to designing it: Clearly state the place, date, and time of the event, and whether special clothing (formal wear, bathing suits, outdoor gear) will be needed. Use of the abbreviation, "R.S.V.P." should *encourage* guests to answer, but be prepared to telephone those who do not respond. And do avoid the error of the unnamed hostess (mentioned in an 1899 etiquette manual) who confused R.S.V.P. with R.I.P., which stands for, "requiescat in pace" (rest in peace) — "a pleasant wish enough, but one her friends were not ready to see used for them."

APRIL FOOLS' DAY DINNER

Teetotaler's Champagne • Poor Man's Caviar

Faux Lobster Stew • Mock Oysters

Lamb's Tongue and Rocket Salad

Mock Cherry Pie

SERVES 4

▼

April Fools' Day is the playful pretext for this gathering. All of the dishes are delicious puns—witty imitations of their more elegant counterparts. Dinner begins with a grape-juice "champagne" toast and an appetizer of eggplant "caviar." (For *haute* foolishness, serve the "caviar" in a real caviar server and the "champagne" in crystal flutes.) The "lobster" stew that follows is actually made with monkfish; and the corn "oysters" served alongside are no less tasty for being oyster free. The salad is a toss of lamb's tongue and rocket—greens more familiarly known as mâche and arugula. For dessert, there's a "cherry" pie filled with cleverly disguised cranberries.

Since many of the dishes are "fishy" (and since the French name for an April fools' prank is *poisson d'avril*—"April fish"), a tabletop suggestive of the shore, awash with cool shades of blue, seashells, and fish-shaped accessories, is appropriate. Offer shell-shaped candies with after-dinner brandy.

Teetotaler's Champagne

Unsweetened white grape juice—available bottled or as a frozen concentrate—has a pleasantly winey flavor. With seltzer or sparkling mineral water added, it makes a light-hearted and nonalcoholic substitute for champagne. If you'd like to serve "pink champagne," simply add a few drops of cranberry juice or purple grape juice.

2 cups unsweetened white grape juice, well chilled

1 cup seltzer or sparkling mineral water

Pour the grape juice into a pitcher and add the seltzer. Pour the mixture into champagne glasses and serve immediately.

Makes 4 servings

In The Art of Entertaining by Jean Walden, published in the Roaring 'Twenties, a fish dinner and bridge party is suggested for "the fishin' season." A low crystal bowl containing a water lily and a few goldfish serves as the centerpiece. The bridge prize is "a reliable brand of canned lobster Newburg . . . decidedly popular in these meatless, maidless days of Spring."

Poor Man's Caviar

This traditional Russian appetizer will never be mistaken for Sevruga or Beluga, but it is a delicious first course and goes very well with the classic caviar accompaniments of toast points and champagne. To make your service even more authentic, place the bowl of caviar on ice, garnish it with lemon wedges, and surround it with dishes of finely chopped egg yolk and egg white.

1½ pounds eggplant
1½ teaspoons salt
About ¼ cup olive oil
1 cup chopped scallions
2 cloves garlic, minced

2 tomatoes, coarsely chopped
⅓ cup chopped parsley
¼ teaspoon oregano
¼ teaspoon pepper
6 thin slices white bread

1. Using a vegetable peeler, pare the eggplant. Cut the eggplant in half lengthwise, then score the cut surfaces and sprinkle them with the salt. Place the eggplant halves on paper towels and set aside for 30 minutes.

2. Squeeze the eggplant and pat it with paper towels to remove as much moisture as possible. Finely chop the eggplant.

3. In a medium skillet, preferably nonstick, heat the oil over medium-high heat. Add the eggplant and sauté until almost browned, about 15 minutes, adding a little more oil if necessary.

4. Add the scallions and garlic, and sauté for 1 to 2 minutes longer. Remove the skillet from the heat and stir in the tomatoes, parsley, oregano, and pepper. Transfer the mixture to a serving bowl, cover, and refrigerate for at least 1 hour, or until the flavors are blended.

5. To serve, toast the bread. Remove the crusts, if you like, and cut each slice of toast diagonally in half. Serve the toast with the eggplant mixture.

4 servings

Faux Lobster Stew, Mock Oysters, and Lamb's Tongue and Rocket Salad

Faux Lobster Stew

Challenge your guests by asking them to identify the main ingredient in this satisfying stew. It is firm, succulent monkfish, also called goosefish or anglerfish, and its meaty texture makes it a fairly convincing—and less expensive—substitute for lobster. Monkfish has long been popular in France, where it is used primarily in stews.

Since it is the names of the foods that give this meal its humor, be sure your dinner guests know what each dish is called. A simple way to enlighten them is by writing the menu on small sheets of notepaper or parchment, rolling them into scrolls, and tying them with ribbons.

¼ cup olive oil
1 cup chopped scallions, white part only
1 cup chopped shallots
3 cloves garlic, minced
2 tablespoons butter
3 tablespoons flour
2 cups coarsely chopped carrots

3 cups canned chicken broth
2 cups dry white wine
¼ cup chopped fresh dill, or 1 tablespoon dried
1 bay leaf
½ teaspoon salt, or to taste
¼ teaspoon white pepper
3 pounds monkfish fillets, cut into 1-inch cubes

1. In a Dutch oven or flameproof casserole, heat the oil over medium heat. Add the scallions, shallots, and garlic, and sauté until softened, about 5 minutes. Add the butter, and when it melts, stir in the flour. Cook, stirring, until the flour is blended into the fat, about 1 minute.

2. Add the carrots, chicken broth, wine, 2 tablespoons of the fresh dill (or all of the dried dill), the bay leaf, salt, and pepper, and stir well. Reduce the heat to medium-low, cover, and simmer until the carrots are tender, about 30 minutes.

3. Add the fish, cover, and simmer until the fish is opaque, about 5 minutes longer. Turn off the heat and let the stew stand, covered, for 5 minutes.

4. Ladle the stew into soup plates and sprinkle each serving with some of the remaining 2 tablespoons fresh dill. *4 servings*

Mock Oysters

Deep-fried corn fritters are sometimes called corn oysters or mock oysters because they resemble fried oysters in size and shape. Of the Green Corn Fritters in her 1871 book, *Common Sense in the Household,* Marion Harland wrote, "Eaten at dinner or breakfast, these always meet with a cordial welcome." Corn cut from the cob is the first choice for this recipe. Thawed frozen corn or even canned corn can be substituted, but either must be drained on paper towels before frying, to prevent spattering.

2 eggs
¼ cup flour
2 tablespoons heavy cream
2 tablespoons chopped chives
½ teaspoon salt

¼ teaspoon pepper
2 cups corn kernels, fresh (about 4 ears) or
    frozen
3 cups vegetable oil

1. In a medium bowl, beat the eggs until light. Add the flour, cream, chives, salt, and pepper. Add the corn and stir until the kernels are evenly coated with batter.

2. In a medium saucepan, heat the oil over medium heat until hot but not smoking (375° on a deep-fat thermometer).

3. Gently place the batter in the hot oil by tablespoonfuls, taking care not to crowd the pan (make two batches, using half the batter for each). Cook the fritters for 1 to 2 minutes on each side, turning once, until both sides are golden brown.

4. Using a slotted spoon, transfer the fritters to paper towels to drain, then place them on a heated platter while you fry the remaining batter.   *4 servings*

Lamb's Tongue and Rocket Salad

Lamb's tongue and rocket are salad greens, often called by other names. Lamb's tongue—also known as lamb's lettuce, mâche, corn salad, or field salad—is a type of wild lettuce, now cultivated for the market. It has downy, tongue-shaped leaves and a mild to slightly sweet flavor. Rocket, or roquette, is more commonly known as arugula. This mildly bitter green is very popular in Italy; its leaves are shaped somewhat like radish leaves. Both greens are very perishable and should not be purchased too far in advance. Arugula is often sold with its roots attached, and lamb's tongue is almost always found this way in the market. To clean these greens, cut off the roots and swish the leaves in a sinkful of water as you would spinach. Both lamb's tongue and arugula can be quite sandy, so rinse the leaves carefully.

Eye-fooling sugar candies shaped and colored like beach-worn seashells and bits of coral make an elegant adjunct to brandy or coffee served after the meal. Molded chocolates in seashell shapes could also be presented with after-dinner drinks.

¼ cup olive oil	¼ teaspoon pepper
¼ cup white wine vinegar	7 cups (loosely packed) rocket
3 tablespoons grainy mustard	4 cups (loosely packed) lamb's tongue
1 teaspoon Worcestershire sauce	1½ cups red cherry tomatoes
1 teaspoon basil	1 cup yellow cherry tomatoes
½ teaspoon salt	

1. In a small bowl, combine the oil, vinegar, mustard, Worcestershire sauce, basil, salt, and pepper, and whisk until well blended.

2. Tear the greens into bite-size pieces and place them in a salad bowl. Halve the tomatoes and add them to the salad. Pour the dressing over the salad and toss gently.

4 servings

Mock Cherry Pie

When cranberries are sweetened and spiced with almond extract, they make a delicious and convincing substitute for the tart red cherries used in old-fashioned cherry pies. Since raisins are naturally sweet, only a small amount of sugar is needed in this recipe. If you can't find unsweetened cranberry juice, use cranberry juice cocktail.

PASTRY
1½ cups flour
1 teaspoon salt
6 tablespoons chilled butter, cut into pieces
¼ cup chilled vegetable shortening, cut into pieces
5 to 8 tablespoons ice water

⅔ cup fresh breadcrumbs
⅓ cup sugar
3 tablespoons unsweetened cranberry juice
½ teaspoon vanilla extract
½ teaspoon almond extract
1 egg yolk
1 tablespoon milk

FILLING AND GLAZE
3 cups fresh or frozen cranberries
2 cups golden raisins

1. Make the pastry: In a large bowl, combine the flour and salt. With a pastry blender or two knives, cut in the butter and shortening until the mixture resembles coarse crumbs.

2. Sprinkle 2 tablespoons of the ice water over the mixture and toss it with a fork. The dough should be just barely moistened, enough so it will hold together when it's formed into a ball. If necessary, add up to 6 tablespoons more water, 1 tablespoon at a time. Separate one-third of the dough. Form both portions of dough into flat disks, wrap them in plastic wrap, and refrigerate for at least 30 minutes.

3. On a lightly floured surface, roll out the larger portion of dough to a 12-inch circle. Fit the dough into a 9-inch glass pie plate. Trim the overhang to an even ½ inch all the way around. Fold the overhang under and score the edge of the crust with the pastry cutter to form a decorative border. Prick the pastry with a fork. Place the pie shell in the freezer to chill for at least 15 minutes before baking.

4. Meanwhile, roll out the remaining dough to a rough 9-inch square, then cut it into ½-inch-wide strips. Working on a baking sheet lined with waxed paper, weave the strips of dough into a lattice. Place the lattice, still on the waxed paper, in the freezer to chill while you make the filling and glaze.

5. Preheat the oven to 450°.

6. Make the filling and glaze: In a large bowl, combine the cranberries, raisins, breadcrumbs, sugar, cranberry juice, and vanilla and almond extracts, and toss gently. In a small bowl, stir together the egg yolk and milk to make the egg glaze.

7. Pour the berry filling into the pie shell. Carefully place the lattice on top of the filling and trim the ends of the lattice strips even with the rim of the crust. Brush the rim and lattice with the egg glaze, and bake for 10 minutes, then reduce the oven temperature to 350° and bake for 30 to 40 minutes longer, or until the crust is golden. Serve the pie warm, or at room temperature.   *Makes one 9-inch pie*

A s described in the 1922 cookbook **A Thousand Ways to Please a Family,** *an April Fools' supper began with a "Dunce Salad" of fruit-filled oranges topped with ice cream cones to resemble students in dunce caps. This was served with "Dunce Diplomas"— rolled sandwiches tied with colored ribbons. For dessert, sponge cake slices were capped with peach halves and whipped cream to masquerade as "First of April Eggs on Toast."*

Mock Cherry Pie

SPRINGTIME TOPIARIES

A. Insert the end of the branch into the Styrofoam ball to a depth of 1 inch. Be careful to mount the ball straight.

B. Using a glue gun, alternately attach pieces of reindeer moss and individual flowers to the ball.

C. Be careful to keep the "trunk" straight as you push it into the oasis. Glue it in place for extra security.

The ancient art of topiary—training and pruning trees or shrubs into formal or fanciful shapes—is the inspiration for this handsome, long-lasting table decoration. Dried reindeer moss and flowers are attached to a Styrofoam ball, which is mounted on a "trunk" and "planted" in a pretty cachepot. For a pleasing, natural look, use a section of a sturdy branch as the trunk. A hot-glue gun makes it easy to attach the flowers and pieces of moss to the foam ball. As you will be holding these small items in your fingers while you work, be careful not to burn yourself; the glue can get extremely hot.

The materials you'll need for this project are widely available. Florists and craft shops offer a variety of dried flowers and mosses. Choose flowers to match the color scheme of your table, or to suggest a holiday theme. Styrofoam balls can be found at craft and hobby shops; oasis (flower-arranging foam) is sold by florists. The directions given are for a 5-inch-diameter topiary; the two smaller trees shown in the photograph were made with 3- and 4-inch Styrofoam balls.

MATERIALS

· Dried roses, strawflowers, or other dried flowers (one 5-inch-diameter topiary will require approximately 3 dozen roses or 30 strawflowers) ·

· Straight branch, about ¾ inch thick and about 12 inches long ·

· Styrofoam ball, 5 inches in diameter ·

· 3½-ounce bag of gray or green reindeer moss ·

· A block of oasis · Flowerpot or cachepot · Small bag of Spanish moss ·

· 36-inch length of ribbon · Scissors · Hot-glue gun ·

◆

DIRECTIONS

1. Cut the stems off the dried flowers just below the flower heads.

2. Place one end of the branch against the Styrofoam ball. Carefully push the end of the branch into the ball to a depth of about 1 inch, being sure to keep the ball straight on the stick (Illustration A).

3. Pull the branch out and coat one end with hot glue. Replace the branch in the hole and hold it for a few seconds until the glue sets.

4. Apply hot glue to the flat side of a piece of reindeer moss and attach it to the Styrofoam ball. Hold the moss in place for a few seconds until the glue sets. In the same manner, glue a flower to the ball next to the moss. Repeat, alternating moss and flowers, until the ball is completely covered; the proportion of moss to flowers is up to you (Illustration B).

5. Cut the block of oasis to fit the pot snugly. Place the bottom end of the branch in the center of the block and mark its outline with a felt-tipped pen. Remove the block from the pot and press the branch into it to a depth of 2 to 3 inches, being careful to keep the topiary straight. Use some hot glue to secure the branch in the block (Illustration C).

6. Return the oasis block and topiary to the pot. Cover the surface of the block with Spanish moss. Tie the ribbon in a bow around the trunk.

EASTER BREAKFAST

Tangerine-Raspberry Juice

Buckwheat-Buttermilk Flapjacks

Creamy Strawberry Spread

Maple-Glazed Sausages

Orange and Blueberry Salad

Egg Braid

SERVES 6

▼

Easter morning is a good time to bring friends and family together for a special breakfast or brunch. Take advantage of the relaxed holiday atmosphere to prepare pancakes, sausages, yeast bread, and other morning treats you may not have time for on hurried weekdays.

The room should glow with the pastels and greens of an early spring garden. Create a cheery arrangement of cut flowers, or bring pots or flats of flowering bulb plants to the table. If your guests include youngsters, be sure that dyed and decorated eggs, baskets of jellybeans, or chocolate rabbits are part of the table decor. The special egg-wreath bread shown on page 116 would make a tempting centerpiece, but you can also bake the bread as a simple braid (as shown here) or substitute a homemade or store-bought coffeecake or sweet yeast bread. Offer a sweet selection of honey, jams, and jellies alongside.

Tangerine-Raspberry Juice

If you want to streamline the preparations, blend a reconstituted 6-ounce can of frozen tangerine juice concentrate with the puréed raspberries instead of squeezing fresh tangerines. Strawberries and orange juice can be combined to make an equally delicious breakfast beverage.

2 packages (10 ounces each) unsweetened   *16 tangerines*
   frozen raspberries, thawed

1. Place the raspberries and their juice in a food processor or blender and process until puréed. Force the mashed berries through a fine sieve set over a bowl to remove the seeds. Transfer the sieved purée to a pitcher.

2. Halve and squeeze the tangerines; strain the juice into the pitcher and stir well. Cover and refrigerate until serving time.

3. Stir the juice mixture to blend it before serving.   *6 servings*

Colored eggs are a natural for brightening the Easter table. These were decorated by a traditional Ukrainian method: patterns are drawn on the shells with melted wax before the eggs are dyed. Use your own favorite technique and display your handiwork in egg cups or baskets.

Buckwheat-Buttermilk Flapjacks

For a mild buckwheat taste, white flour is used in a three-to-one proportion to light buckwheat flour in this recipe. If you are fond of the assertive flavor of buckwheat, increase the proportion of buckwheat to white flour, or use dark, rather than light, buckwheat flour.

1½ cups all-purpose flour   *½ teaspoon salt*
½ cup light buckwheat flour   *2 cups buttermilk*
2 tablespoons sugar   *2 eggs, lightly beaten*
1½ teaspoons baking powder   *4 tablespoons butter, melted*
1 teaspoon baking soda   *About 2 tablespoons vegetable oil*

1. In a large bowl, stir together the flours, sugar, baking powder, baking soda, and salt, and make a well in the center.

2. In a medium bowl, stir together the buttermilk, eggs, and the melted butter. Pour the egg mixture into the dry ingredients and stir just until blended; do not overmix.

3. Lightly oil a griddle or heavy skillet and heat it over medium heat. Drop the batter by scant ¼ cups onto the griddle and cook the pancakes until small bubbles appear on the tops, then turn them and cook until golden, about 3 minutes per side. Add more oil to the skillet as necessary.   *6 servings*

Creamy Strawberry Spread

This luscious pancake topping, which can also be spread on hot toast, quick breads, waffles, or French toast, will keep for up to a week in the refrigerator. Fresh strawberries are recommended for this recipe, but it can also be made with unsweetened frozen strawberries, thawed and well drained. For an interesting variation, flavor the spread with tangerine zest and juice instead of lemon.

6 ounces fresh strawberries, or unsweetened frozen strawberries, thawed
About 3 tablespoons superfine sugar or confectioners' sugar

2 teaspoons lemon juice
1 teaspoon grated lemon zest
1 package (3 ounces) cream cheese, softened to room temperature

1. In a small bowl, mash the strawberries with a fork. Stir in sugar to taste and the lemon juice and zest; set aside.
2. In another small bowl, beat the cream cheese until soft and smooth. Add the strawberry mixture and stir until combined. Cover the bowl and refrigerate until needed.

Makes about 1 cup

Spring flowers grown from bulbs, such as crocuses, tulips, narcissuses, or lilies, can come to the table in the flats or pots in which they were originally planted. For a real country-garden feeling, fill out the planter with grass, or cover the surface of the soil with moss.

Maple-Glazed Sausages

Maple syrup, which is made in the spring, deserves a place in springtime meals. Here, it adds a mellow sweetness to these breakfast sausages. Although they are broiled rather than pan-fried, the sausages must still be watched and turned often so that the sugar in the maple syrup does not scorch.

18 small breakfast sausages (about 1 ounce each)

⅓ cup maple syrup
2 tablespoons chopped parsley, for garnish

1. Preheat the broiler. Line a broiler pan with foil.
2. Prick each sausage several times with a fork. Precook the sausages in a small pan of simmering water for 2 to 3 minutes; drain and pat dry with paper towels.
3. Place the sausages on a rack over the foil-lined pan and brush them with maple syrup. Broil the sausages 4 inches from the heat, turning and basting them frequently, for 6 minutes, or until golden brown.
4. Transfer the sausages to a serving platter and sprinkle them with the parsley.

6 servings

Orange and Blueberry Salad

As attractive as it is delicious, this combination of blueberries and oranges can be eaten as a first course, as a side dish with the pancakes and sausage, or as a dessert. If children are joining you for this meal, combine the fruit and marmalade and set aside a portion of this mixture for them; then add the liqueur to the remainder.

12 navel oranges
2 pints blueberries

⅓ cup orange marmalade
¼ cup orange liqueur

1. Peel the oranges, removing all of the white pith. Working over a bowl to catch the juices, separate the oranges into segments, removing the membranes.
2. Add the blueberries, marmalade, and liqueur to the oranges, and toss until combined. Cover the bowl and refrigerate until serving time.   *6 servings*

Orange and Blueberry Salad

Egg Braid

For directions on shaping this rich, golden egg bread into a traditional wreath-shaped braid studded with colored eggs, see An Easter Egg Ring, pages 116-117.

½ cup lukewarm (105° to 115°) water

1 package active dry yeast

⅓ cup sugar

About 5½ cups flour

2 teaspoons ground cardamom

1½ teaspoons salt

3 whole eggs plus 1 egg, separated

½ cup lukewarm (105° to 115°) milk,
  plus 1 tablespoon milk

4 tablespoons butter, melted

1 tablespoon poppy seeds or
  sesame seeds

1. Place the water in a small bowl and sprinkle the yeast over it. Stir in a pinch of the sugar and let the mixture stand until the yeast begins to foam, about 5 minutes.

2. Meanwhile, in a medium bowl, stir together 2 cups of the flour, the remaining sugar, the cardamom, and salt, and make a well in the center. In a small bowl, lightly beat the three eggs and the white of the fourth egg. Place the remaining egg yolk in a small bowl, cover with plastic wrap, and refrigerate until needed.

3. Stir the beaten eggs, yeast mixture, the ½ cup of lukewarm milk, and the butter into the dry ingredients. Stir in 2½ to 3 cups of the flour and continue stirring until the mixture forms a dough.

4. Transfer the dough to a lightly floured surface and knead it until smooth and elastic, about 10 minutes, adding up to ½ cup more flour, if necessary. Form the dough into a ball and place it in a large greased bowl; turn the dough to coat the surface. Set aside, uncovered, in a warm, draft-free place, and let rise until doubled in bulk, 1 to 1¼ hours.

5. Lightly grease two baking sheets.

6. Punch the dough down, then transfer it to a lightly floured surface. Knead the dough for 1 minute, then divide it in half.

7. Wrap and set aside one piece of dough while you form the first braid: Pinch off one-third of the dough. Divide the remaining, larger piece into three portions and roll each into an 18-inch rope about ¾ inch thick. Flatten the ropes to a 1-inch width. Lay the three ropes, side by side, on one of the prepared baking sheets, pinch them together at one end, and braid them. Pinch the other end of the braid together.

8. Divide the smaller piece of dough into two portions and roll each into a 15-inch rope. Twist these two ropes together, pinch the ends together, and lay them on top of the larger braid. Cover the loaf with a slightly dampened kitchen towel and set aside in a warm, draft-free place to rise until almost doubled in bulk, 30 to 45 minutes. Meanwhile, form the second portion of dough in the same fashion.

9. Preheat the oven to 400°. In a small bowl, beat the reserved egg yolk with the remaining 1 tablespoon milk to make a glaze.

10. Brush the tops of the braids with the glaze and sprinkle them with the poppy seeds. Bake for 15 to 20 minutes, or until the breads are golden brown. Cool the braids on the baking sheets for 10 minutes, then transfer them to a rack to cool completely before slicing.

Makes two 16-inch braids

The Art of Entertaining, *published in 1927, suggested a children's Easter party:* "Each child is given a basket upon his arrival labeled with his name; for the first thing is the Easter-egg hunt, without which no party is complete. It is more fun if there are eggs of all kinds and sizes hidden about the house. Even big china eggs as 'prizes' are wonderful in the eyes of the child who finds one!"

AN EASTER EGG RING

Bread has been symbolic of sustenance and survival since ancient times, so it seems only natural that special breads have come to be part of the celebration of religious and seasonal feasts and festivals. A braided Easter bread with whole eggs tucked into its rich dough is one such creation. For centuries, breads similar to this one have been baked in Greece, Italy, and parts of northern Europe.

To make this edible Easter centerpiece, first color three hard-cooked eggs. If you'd like to try natural dyes, simmer a handful of red or yellow onion skins or red cabbage leaves in a small pan of boiling water for about 15 minutes. Add the eggs and a tablespoonful of vinegar, and simmer for about 20 minutes longer; let the eggs cool in the dye. Prepare the dough for the Egg Braid (page 115) through Step 6, then divide each piece of dough into three 24-inch ropes. Flatten the ropes slightly, pinch them together at one end, and braid. Join the ends to form a ring. Tuck the eggs part-way into the braided dough, then cover and let rise as directed in Step 8 of the recipe. Brush the glaze only on the dough (not on the eggs) and sprinkle the dough with sesame or poppy seeds, if desired. Repeat with the second portion of dough and bake as directed.

You will need three 24-inch ropes to form one braid. Gently press on each rope to flatten it slightly.

Lay the ropes side by side on a greased baking sheet, then pinch them together at one end and braid them.

Join the ends to form a ring, then partially insert the eggs between the strands of dough.

SOUTHWESTERN GRADUATION BUFFET

Zesty Guacamole · *Chunky Black Bean Dip*

Fresh Salsa · *Green Chili-Corn Pudding*

Chicken Fajitas with Bell Peppers

Tropical Fruit Salad · *Sunny Sangria*

New Mexican Chocolate Cake

SERVES 20 OR MORE

▼

Southwestern foods are ideal for entertaining a crowd; here, presented as a bountiful buffet, their lively flavors suit the soaring spirits of high-school or college graduates. The informal setting, accented with chunky pottery (any vintage will do) and textiles in vivid Southwestern hues, contributes to the fiesta atmosphere; add a piñata, strings of colored lights, and a forest of miniature cacti to enhance the Tex-Mex mood.

This menu is simple to prepare; no exotic ingredients are required for these foods, and teenagers equipped with basic kitchen skills could cook the meal themselves. The main dish is chicken fajitas—strips of juicy grilled chicken and vegetables. These are placed in flour tortillas and topped with condiments, then rolled up for easy eating. The dessert is a crowd-pleasing chocolate cake that can be iced with a creamy coffee icing and inscribed as you wish, or decorated to resemble a Navajo blanket, as shown on page 126.

Zesty Guacamole

Lime juice and coriander are key seasonings in this appetizer. If the avocados you buy are not ripe (they should yield to gentle pressure at the stem end), place them in a paper bag with an apple and leave them at room temperature to ripen for a few days.

Mexican food was new to most Americans in 1904, when Entertainments For All Seasons *was published. The Mexican luncheon—"a fad that originated in California"—was a novelty. If the "serapes, sombreros . . . and cacti blossoms that the Pacific coast hostess uses to give a Mexican setting" were not available, one could adorn the dining room with "palms, rubber plants, plain unbaked pottery . . . and a liberal use of the Mexican colors."*

6 ripe avocados, peeled and pitted
¾ cup finely chopped red onion
3 cloves garlic, minced
⅓ cup lime juice
⅓ cup sour cream

⅓ cup chopped fresh coriander
1 tablespoon chili powder
1½ teaspoons salt
¾ teaspoon black pepper
½ teaspoon hot pepper sauce, or to taste

1. Place the avocados in a large bowl and mash them lightly with a fork, leaving them slightly chunky.

2. Add the onion, garlic, lime juice, sour cream, coriander, chili powder, salt, black pepper, and hot pepper sauce, and mix until well blended. If not serving immediately, lay a sheet of heavy-duty plastic wrap directly on the surface of the guacamole, cover the bowl, and refrigerate. *Makes about 6 cups*

Chunky Black Bean Dip

If you'd like to use dried beans for this recipe, prepare them as follows: Place 3 cups of dried beans in a medium saucepan with water to cover by 2 inches (do not add salt at this point; it toughens the beans). Bring to a boil and boil for 2 minutes, then remove the pan from the heat, cover, and let stand for 1 hour. Drain the beans, add fresh cold water to cover, and bring to a boil over medium-high heat. Reduce the heat to low and simmer, partially covered, until the beans are tender, 1 to 1½ hours.

½ pound bacon (8 to 12 slices)
3 cups chopped scallions
12 cloves garlic, minced
¼ cup chili powder
1 tablespoon ground cumin

6 cups cooked black beans
¾ cup olive oil
6 to 9 drops hot pepper sauce
1½ teaspoons salt
¾ teaspoon black pepper

1. In a large skillet, cook the bacon over medium heat until crisp, about 10 minutes. Reserving 3 tablespoons of fat in the skillet, drain the bacon on paper towels; crumble and set aside.

2. Add the scallions and garlic to the skillet and sauté over medium heat until the scallions are softened but not browned, about 5 minutes. Add the chili powder and cumin, and cook, stirring, for 1 minute; set aside.

3. Place the beans in a large bowl and mash them lightly with a fork or a potato masher. Add the oil, hot pepper sauce, salt, and black pepper, and mix well. Stir in the scallion mixture and the reserved bacon. *Makes about 6 cups*

Fresh Salsa

This flavorful tomato salsa can be used as a dip for tortilla chips or as a condiment for the fajitas. It should be made at least 30 minutes ahead of time to allow the flavors to blend, and can also be prepared a day in advance and refrigerated. Serve any leftover salsa with cold chicken or with scrambled eggs. For how to handle chilies, see A Primer on Chilies, pages 30-31.

3 large tomatoes (about 1½ pounds)
2 small red onions, finely chopped
4 cloves garlic, minced
2 tablespoons seeded, finely chopped
  jalapeño peppers

½ cup chopped fresh coriander
½ cup red wine vinegar
2 tablespoons olive oil
1 teaspoon salt
½ teaspoon black pepper

1. Core and coarsely chop the tomatoes. If they are very watery, drain the excess liquid.

2. Place the chopped tomatoes in a large bowl, add the onions, garlic, jalapeños, coriander, vinegar, oil, salt, and black pepper, and mix until well blended.

3. Let the salsa stand for at least 30 minutes before serving.   *Makes about 5 cups*

Zesty Guacamole, Chunky Black Bean Dip, Fresh Salsa, and tortilla chips

Green Chili-Corn Pudding

Although made with chilies and pepper jack (Monterey jack cheese flecked with bits of jalapeño), this pudding is relatively mild and provides a pleasant contrast to the spicier foods in this menu. To free the oven for cooking the fajitas, bake the corn pudding about thirty minutes ahead of time and cover it with foil to keep it warm.

1½ cups yellow cornmeal
2 teaspoons sugar
1 teaspoon salt
1 teaspoon baking powder
½ teaspoon pepper
2 packages (10 ounces each) frozen corn
kernels, thawed

4 cans (4 ounces each) chopped mild
green chilies, drained
4 cups (2 pints) light cream or half-and-half
6 eggs, lightly beaten
4 cups grated pepper jack cheese (about
1 pound)
⅔ cup chopped fresh coriander

1. Preheat the oven to 350°. Butter a 3-quart casserole or baking dish.
2. In a medium bowl, stir together the cornmeal, sugar, salt, baking powder, and pepper.
3. In a large bowl, stir together the corn, green chilies, cream, and eggs. Stir in the cornmeal mixture, then add 3 cups of the cheese and the coriander. Pour the mixture into the prepared casserole dish and sprinkle the remaining cheese on top.
4. Bake for 1½ hours, or until the pudding is set and the top is golden. If the edges seem to be browning too quickly, cover them with foil.   *20 servings*

Here is a glimpse of graduation parties circa 1910, from A Handbook of Hospitality for Town and Country: "Every collegian wishes to ask some friends to the graduation festivities, no matter on how simple a scale these may be. . . . Our Senior will probably wish to offer some simple refreshments to his friends. . . . Sandwiches, cake, lemonade and punch will be sufficient, with tea or coffee if the weather is cold or damp."

Chicken Fajitas with Bell Peppers

"Fajitas" is the Mexican term for skirt steak, which is traditionally the main ingredient of this dish. However, this rolled-tortilla meal can also be made—as it is here—with strips of chicken, or with grilled fish or seafood. The accompaniments included in the recipe—onion rings, olives, shredded lettuce, and sour cream—allow plenty of choices for custom-garnishing each portion; but your guests can also spoon the guacamole, black bean dip, and salsa onto their fajitas.

2½ cups lemon juice
1¼ cups olive oil
1⅔ cups chopped fresh coriander
15 cloves garlic, minced
5 teaspoons oregano
5 teaspoons basil
2½ teaspoons salt
1¼ teaspoons black pepper
6 pounds skinless, boneless
chicken breast halves

10 red bell peppers, thinly sliced
40 flour tortillas

CONDIMENTS
2 large red onions, thinly sliced
3 cups sour cream
4 cups pitted small black olives
10 cups shredded Romaine lettuce

The graduation party meal

1. In a large, nonreactive bowl, combine the lemon juice, oil, coriander, garlic, oregano, basil, salt, and black pepper. Add the chicken and bell peppers, and toss until well coated with the marinade. Cover the bowl with plastic wrap and marinate for at least 4 hours, or overnight, in the refrigerator, tossing a few times if possible.

2. Preheat the broiler. Line a large broiler pan with foil.

3. Working in batches, place the chicken breasts and bell peppers on the broiler pan and broil 4 to 6 inches from the heat for 4 to 6 minutes per side, or until the chicken is cooked through and the peppers are limp.

4. Meanwhile, stack the tortillas, wrap them in foil, and warm them in the oven or in a toaster oven. Wrap each batch of chicken and bell peppers in foil to keep it warm.

5. Cut the chicken into thin strips on the diagonal. Place the chicken, bell peppers, and tortillas on warm serving platters and serve with the condiments. Each diner places chicken strips and peppers in the center of a tortilla, adds condiments, and then folds the tortilla around the filling.

Makes about 40 fajitas

Tropical Fruit Salad

Although the fruits used in this salad are tropical, they are no longer as exotic as they once were; most are now sold at greengrocers or supermarkets. If your local stores do not have papayas, mangos, or kiwi fruit, simply use more honeydew or pineapple, or substitute cubes of cantaloupe, peach, or nectarine.

Miniature cactus plants bring the landscape of the Southwest to your tabletop. The terra-cotta pots already have a desert flavor, which can be enhanced by stamping them with simple Indian-inspired patterns. You can cut the stamps from art-gum erasers or potatoes, then dip them into acrylic paints before applying.

¾ cup lime juice
¾ cup orange juice concentrate
6 tablespoons honey
6 cups cubed honeydew (1 medium melon)
6 cups fresh pineapple slices, quartered
   (1 medium pineapple)

3 cups sliced kiwi fruit (about 8 kiwi fruit)
3 cups cubed papaya (1 medium papaya)
1½ cups cubed mango (2 mangos)
1 cup grated fresh coconut, or unsweetened
   shredded coconut
¾ cup chopped fresh mint

1. In a small bowl, combine the lime juice, orange juice concentrate, and honey, and stir until well blended.

2. In a large serving bowl, combine the honeydew, pineapple, kiwi fruit, papaya, mango, and ¾ cup of the coconut. Pour on the lime-juice mixture and toss until the fruit is well coated. Cover and refrigerate for at least 1 hour.

3. Sprinkle the fruit salad with the mint and the remaining ¼ cup coconut, and serve. *Makes about 18 cups*

Sunny Sangria

Sangria, which originated in Spain, is also popular in Mexico and Texas. It is traditionally made by adding cut-up fresh fruit to a robust red wine. This alcohol-free version is based on pineapple juice and white grape juice.

4 lemons
4 limes
3 oranges
1 pink grapefruit
1 quart pineapple juice

1 bottle (24 ounces) unsweetened white
   grape juice
1 red apple, thinly sliced
1 cup strawberries, lightly crushed, plus whole
   strawberries for garnish

1. Wash and thinly slice one lemon, one lime, and one orange, and place the slices in a punch bowl. Halve and squeeze the grapefruit and the remaining lemons, limes, and oranges, and pour the juices into the punch bowl.

2. Add the pineapple and grape juices to the bowl, then add the apple slices and crushed strawberries, and stir well. Cover the bowl and refrigerate the sangria for at least 2 hours.

3. Just before serving, stir the sangria again and add the whole strawberries.
Makes about 4 quarts

New Mexican Chocolate Cake

This rich chocolate cake can be frosted with a simple coffee icing and inscribed with wishes for the happy graduates. Or, it can be decorated to resemble a Navajo Indian weaving: See A Navajo Blanket Cake on pages 126-127 for step-by-step directions.

CAKE

2 cups flour

¼ cup unsweetened cocoa powder

2 teaspoons cinnamon

3 sticks (12 ounces) butter, cut into pieces

8 ounces semisweet chocolate

1 cup milk

1 teaspoon powdered instant espresso

4 eggs, separated

1½ cups sugar

1 teaspoon vanilla extract

½ teaspoon salt

ICING

⅓ cup heavy cream

4 tablespoons butter, softened to room temperature

3 cups confectioners' sugar

1½ teaspoons powdered instant espresso dissolved in 2 teaspoons hot water

When the occasion calls for presents or favors, wrapping them in the colors of the party decor transforms them into distinctive accents. Other attractive trimmings include: bandannas, tassels, Southwestern stickers and stamps, and natural materials such as dried flowers and dried chilies.

1. Preheat the oven to 350°. Butter a 15 x 10 x 2-inch cake pan, line the bottom with buttered waxed paper, and flour the waxed paper.

2. Make the cake: In a medium bowl, stir together the flour, cocoa powder, and cinnamon; set aside.

3. In a small heavy saucepan, combine the butter, chocolate, milk, and espresso powder. Cook over low heat, stirring until smooth. Set aside to cool slightly.

4. In a medium bowl, beat the egg yolks and sugar until pale and lemon-colored. Add the cooled chocolate mixture and the vanilla, and beat until blended.

5. In another bowl, using an electric mixer, beat the egg whites and salt until stiff peaks form.

6. Gradually add the dry ingredients to the batter, beating well after each addition. Fold in the beaten egg whites.

7. Spread the batter evenly in the prepared pan. Rap the pan once or twice on the counter to remove any air pockets. Bake for about 30 minutes, or until a toothpick inserted in the center of the cake comes out clean.

8. Cool the cake in the pan for 10 minutes, then carefully turn it out onto the rack to cool completely. (The cake may also be iced and served in the pan.)

9. Meanwhile, make the icing: In a medium bowl, beat together the cream and butter until smooth. Gradually add the confectioners' sugar, beating until smooth and fluffy. Add the espresso mixture, and beat until blended.

10. Spread the icing over the top and sides of the cake.

Makes one 15 x 10-inch sheet cake

A NAVAJO BLANKET CAKE

Smooth the coffee icing by placing the edge of a metal ruler or straightedge at one end of the cake and drawing it toward you.

Cut a notched diamond shape from stiff paper. Holding it just above the surface of the icing, trace around the pattern with a skewer or toothpick.

Lay the ruler alongside the cake and, using a skewer or toothpick, measure and mark the placement of the stripes on the long sides of the cake.

Using two cups of equal size, place one on each side of the cake. Rest the ruler on the cups, and make stripes by tracing lines with a skewer.

Using a #44 piping tip, pipe stripes of chocolate icing over the traced lines. Try to exert firm, steady pressure to create smooth stripes of even width.

Using a #45 tip, pipe short strokes of chocolate icing around the diamonds to give the effect of a woven pattern. Complete the design with red accents.

A decorated cake can be the highlight of any party. Here, a Navajo blanket pattern has been adapted in icing for a Southwestern-theme party. The instructions that follow explain how to decorate the cake; use the large photograph as a guide to the design.

Bake the New Mexican Chocolate Cake (page 125) as directed through Step 8, then make a double recipe of icing (Step 9). Measure out a 1-cup portion and a ½-cup portion of the icing, and set aside in separate bowls.

Place 4 ounces of semisweet chocolate, cut into pieces, in a double boiler set over hot, not simmering, water. Melt the chocolate, stirring until smooth. Let cool slightly, then stir the chocolate into the 1-cup portion of icing. Blend ½ teaspoon of scarlet paste food coloring (available from cake-decorating suppliers) into the ½-cup portion of icing.

Ice the cake with the reserved coffee icing. Using a pattern, trace a diamond at the center and half-diamonds at the edges of the cake. Then measure and mark the placement of the stripes. Fill one pastry bag with chocolate icing and another with scarlet icing. Use a #44 (ribbon) piping tip for the broad stripes, a #4 (round) tip for the narrow stripes, and a #45 (ribbon) tip for the short strokes around the diamonds. (If you do not have two pastry bags and duplicate piping tips, wash the bag and tips before changing icing colors.)

FOUR

Summer

*a time for dining
out of doors in country
comfort*

A swath of emerald lawn, a shady tree, and the company of friends—what better can life hold? Perhaps a morsel—or more—of something delicious to eat. "To enjoy thoroughly a summer one should understand the picnic," wrote Caroline French Benton in her 1911 book, *Easy Entertaining*. "Too many who might know all about it never really find out its delights." Whether it is for an Independence Day outing, with flavors bright as fireworks, or a nostalgic Victorian-style box-social picnic, hardly anyone will refuse an invitation to dine *al fresco*.

If you have a garden, live in the country, or are within reach of a park, you know that even the simplest meal has a special savor when eaten out of doors. The menus in this chapter, replete with recipes for honey-baked chicken, barbecued steaks, peach pie, and other seasonal favorites, are enhanced by summer sunshine. To beat the heat, offer an afternoon tea, reminiscent of an old-fashioned cakewalk, in the breezy shade of verandah or porch.

When gardens are in full fruit and flower, summer tables are at their best.

FOURTH OF JULY
PICNIC

Lemon-Herb Roasted Chicken

Shrimp and Avocado Salad · Cornbread Salad

Summer Fruit Bowl with Minted Yogurt Dressing

Peasant Bread · Herbed Cream Cheese

Sparkling Fruit Punch

Butterscotch-Fudge Brownies

Black Cow Sodas

S E R V E S 8

▼

Celebrate the Glorious Fourth with a backyard picnic whose bright colors and fresh flavors rival the fireworks. As the main course, bowls of three summery salads surround lemony roasted chicken. Country condiments, such as watermelon-rind or bread-and-butter pickles, provide a pleasantly homey touch. For dessert, butterscotch brownies are a new twist on a classic; for an all-American accompaniment, mix up some soda-fountain drinks. To learn how to make a Black Cow and other old-fashioned beverages, see A Soda-Fountain Sampler, page 138.

The color scheme is obvious—and easy to achieve: If you have white dishes, just add red and blue accessories (keep in mind that any red pieces you buy can reappear at Christmas). Or serve the meal on reusable plastic picnicware.

Lemon-Herb Roasted Chicken

Here lemons, onions, and bay leaves are placed inside broilers, then the birds are rubbed all over with a blend of oil, garlic, lemon zest, and herbs to give them a fine flavor and a crisp, savory skin. Chicken cooked this way is delicious whether it is eaten hot, warm, or cold. The size and number of chickens you will need depends on how many people you are serving; just increase the seasonings as necessary. Once you've added this recipe to your list of "regulars," you will probably want to cook an extra broiler every time you make it, so that you can enjoy the leftovers in sandwiches or salads the next day.

Herbs planted in sponge-painted pots provide both decoration and subtle fragrance at the table. You can tuck miniature paper flags—or placecards—into the pots, and send the plants home with your guests after the picnic.

2 lemons
2 small onions, halved
2 bay leaves
2 teaspoons salt
2 teaspoons pepper

Two 3-pound broiler chickens
½ cup olive oil
6 cloves garlic, minced
½ cup chopped parsley
2 teaspoons thyme

1. Preheat the oven to 425°.
2. Grate enough zest from the lemons to measure 4 teaspoons. Cut the lemons in half; set aside.
3. Place 2 lemon halves, 2 onion halves, 1 bay leaf, and ½ teaspoon each of salt and pepper in the cavity of each chicken. Place the chickens, breast-side up, in a roasting pan.
4. In a small bowl, stir together the oil, lemon zest, remaining 1 teaspoon each salt and pepper, the garlic, parsley, and thyme. Spread the oil mixture over the chickens, then roast them for 15 minutes.
5. Reduce the oven temperature to 350° and roast the chickens for 1 hour longer, or until an instant-reading meat thermometer inserted into the thickest part of the thigh registers 170° and the juices run clear when the same area is pierced with a sharp knife. Baste with the remaining oil mixture during the last 30 minutes.
6. Remove the chickens from the oven and let rest for 5 to 10 minutes before carving. *8 servings*

Shrimp and Avocado Salad

If necessary, you can substitute large or jumbo shrimp for the baby shrimp; shell, devein, and cook them, then cut each one into thirds.

1 cup sour cream
½ cup white wine vinegar
¼ cup chopped fresh coriander
2 teaspoons Dijon mustard
1 teaspoon salt
1 teaspoon pepper
¼ teaspoon hot pepper sauce
1 pound cooked baby shrimp

2 avocados, peeled and cubed
3 medium tomatoes, cubed
1 large yellow bell pepper, diced
1 large green bell pepper, diced
1 can (4 ounces) chopped mild green
    chilies, drained
⅓ cup minced chives or scallions

1. In a small bowl, whisk together the sour cream, vinegar, coriander, mustard, salt, pepper, and hot pepper sauce.

2. In a large serving bowl, combine the shrimp, avocados, tomatoes, bell peppers, and chilies. Pour the dressing over the salad and toss gently until well mixed. Sprinkle the salad with the chives and serve.   *Makes about 11 cups*

Dime stores and novelty shops are great sources of accessories for your Independence Day table. Flags of all sizes, fans, bunting, and streamers will help create a real party atmosphere. Keep them from year to year so you always have a ready supply.

Cornbread Salad

The crisp cubes of cornbread in this salad are lighter tasting than traditional croutons because they are not sautéed in fat. They do, however, absorb enough of the dressing to take on a pleasant tang. Use your own recipe for an 8-inch square cornbread, or try the one included in the recipe for Sausage Cornbread Stuffing (page 44).

8-inch square loaf of cornbread,
    cubed (6 cups)
⅓ cup olive oil
¼ cup lemon juice
¼ cup chopped fresh mint
2 teaspoons dry mustard
1 teaspoon ground coriander

½ teaspoon salt
¼ teaspoon black pepper
6 cups romaine lettuce, torn into
    bite-size pieces
1 large red bell pepper, cut into
    ½-inch squares
1 small red onion, thinly sliced

1. Preheat the oven to 250°.

2. Spread the cornbread cubes on an ungreased baking sheet and bake for 1 hour, or until crisp and dry but not browned. Set aside to cool.

3. In a small bowl, whisk together the oil, lemon juice, mint, mustard, coriander, salt, and black pepper; set aside.

4. In a serving bowl, combine the romaine, bell pepper, onion, and cornbread cubes. Pour the dressing over the salad and toss gently.   *Makes about 10 cups*

Summer Fruit Bowl with Minted Yogurt Dressing

When you combine an assortment of lush summer fruits, their flavors enhance each other and produce an even richer bouquet. The ingredients can be varied according to what is at its peak in your area; choose from the many varieties of plums, melons, and berries that ripen in July.

1 cantaloupe (about 2¼ pounds)
1 pint blueberries
1 pint strawberries
2 medium plums
2 medium nectarines
2 medium peaches

2 tablespoons lime juice
2 cups plain yogurt
⅓ cup honey
⅓ cup chopped fresh mint
1 teaspoon vanilla extract

1. Cut the cantaloupe into 1-inch cubes, or scoop it out with a melon baller. Place the melon in a large serving bowl. Add the blueberries and strawberries.

2. Cut the plums into ½-inch slices and add them to the bowl.

3. Cut the nectarines and peaches into ½-inch slices and sprinkle them with the lime juice. Add them to the bowl and toss gently.

4. In a small bowl, whisk together the yogurt, honey, mint, and vanilla. Serve the fruit salad with the yogurt dressing on the side.

Makes about 10 cups

Herbed Cream Cheese

Serve a fairly dense bread with this flavorful cheese mixture. A staunch Swiss-style peasant bread, chewy Westphalian pumpernickel, or a hearty whole-grain loaf are some possible choices. Sturdy crackers, breadsticks, or cut-up raw vegetables would also make suitable accompaniments.

2 packages (8 ounces each) cream cheese,
*   softened to room temperature*
½ cup sour cream
1 cup finely chopped scallions (2 bunches)
6 tablespoons finely chopped parsley

1 teaspoon basil
1 teaspoon oregano
1 teaspoon salt
½ teaspoon pepper

1. In a medium bowl, beat the cream cheese and sour cream until smoothly blended. Stir in the scallions and parsley.

2. Add the basil and oregano to the cream cheese mixture. Stir in the salt and pepper. Cover the bowl and refrigerate the mixture for at least 2 hours, or until the flavors are well blended. Allow the mixture to come to room temperature before serving.

Makes about 3 cups

The Art of Entertaining, *published in 1927, outlines an Independence Day outing for rowdy, fun-loving boys. "Because most fathers and mothers rather dread the Fourth, here is a suggestion . . . which combines a picnic, fireworks, a campfire, games, a bit o' swimmin', and a sane Fourth, all in one. The Host and Hostess might be any foresighted father and mother who want to make this day a glorious one for their sons, and others as well."*

Cornbread Salad, Shrimp and Avocado Salad, and Summer Fruit Bowl with Minted Yogurt Dressing

Sparkling Fruit Punch

Unsweetened cranberry juice can be found in health food stores, but cranberry juice cocktail can be substituted, if necessary. To make a decorative ice ring to float in a punch bowl, half-fill a ring mold with punch and freeze it. Arrange a layer of fruit slices on top of the frozen punch, then pour in just enough punch to cover the fruit and freeze the mold again. Finally, fill the mold to the top with punch and freeze it solid. To unmold, dip the ring mold very briefly into hot water. Edible flowers can also be frozen into the ice mold.

3 cups unsweetened apple juice
2½ cups unsweetened white grape juice
1 cup unsweetened cranberry juice

1 cup fresh lime juice (8 to 10 limes)
1 quart gingerale or sparkling water (optional)
Lemon or lime slices, for garnish (optional)

1. In a large pitcher, stir together the apple, grape, cranberry, and lime juices.
2. Add gingerale or sparkling water to the pitcher of punch, or serve it separately. Garnish with lemon or lime slices, if desired.   *Makes about 7½ cups*

Black Cow Sodas (page 138) and Butterscotch-Fudge Brownies

Butterscotch-Fudge Brownies

The appealing flavor of butterscotch comes from a simple blending of butter and brown sugar. In this recipe, a layer of butterscotch batter is topped with a fudgy brownie batter, then the two are swirled together to produce irresistible marbleized bar cookies. The recipe can be doubled, if necessary, and—should you choose to make them in advance—the brownies freeze well.

1 cup flour
1½ teaspoons baking powder
⅔ cup plus 3 tablespoons butter
2 cups (packed) light brown sugar
4 whole eggs plus 1 egg yolk

2½ teaspoons vanilla extract
1½ cups chopped walnuts
3 ounces semisweet chocolate,
   broken into pieces
2 tablespoons heavy cream

1. Preheat the oven to 350°. Line a 9-inch square baking pan with foil and lightly butter the foil.

2. In a small bowl, stir together the flour and baking powder; set aside.

3. In a small saucepan, melt ⅔ cup of the butter over medium-low heat. Add the sugar and stir constantly until the sugar dissolves, 10 to 12 minutes. Pour the mixture into a large bowl and let cool until tepid.

4. Beat the whole eggs, one at a time, into the cooled butter mixture, beating well after each addition. Beat in 2 teaspoons of the vanilla. Beat in the dry ingredients, then fold in the walnuts. Pour the batter into the prepared baking pan and spread it evenly with a rubber spatula.

5. In a heavy saucepan, over medium-low heat, melt the chocolate with the remaining 3 tablespoons butter. Beat in the cream and the remaining ½ teaspoon vanilla, then remove the pan from the heat and whisk in the remaining egg yolk.

6. Drizzle the chocolate mixture over the batter in the pan. Pull a knife through the batter to marbleize the butterscotch and chocolate batters. Bake for 1 hour and 15 minutes, or until a cake tester inserted in the center comes out clean.

7. Let the cake cool in the pan on a rack before cutting into squares.

Makes 9 squares

Veranda luncheons were endorsed with enthusiasm in the 1911 book **Easy Entertaining**. *"Happy is the woman who possesses a veranda! She has at once an ideal living room, adorned, doubtless, with gay chintz pillows, window-boxes, and decorative awnings, and a dining room where she may entertain with a certain atmosphere of novelty which even the most attractive dining room indoors must lack."*

A SODA-FOUNTAIN SAMPLER

Have you tasted a Black Cow lately? Sipped a Honey Dew Frappe, Grape Glacé, or Cherry Phosphate? If these names mean anything to you, they probably bring back fond memories of the soda fountain, once a fixture of small-town pharmacies and big-city lunch spots. There, businessmen and society matrons could refresh themselves in a friendly, wholesome atmosphere; at the fountain, two youngsters could linger over a single soda served with two straws. The fountain's counter was a stage on which fizzy, multicolored wonders were created. Soda jerks—alchemists of ice cream, essences, and extracts —presented their concoctions with practiced patter and theatrical fillips (such as tossing ice cream from the scoop to a glass held at arm's length).

Although the soda fountain had its heyday from 1900 through the 1940s, the ice cream soda dates back to the 19th century. In the late 1830s, carbonated water mixed with flavored syrup was sold at drugstore fountains; later, sweet cream was added for a richer drink. In 1874, a fountain proprietor substituted ice cream for the cream, and the new combination was an immediate success.

By the turn of the century, the soda fountain flourished in all its glory, with a marble countertop, mirrored backbar, stained-glass lampshades, and brilliant nickeled pumps. Fountain manuals such as *The American Soda Book* fulfilled the constant demand for novel syrups, sodas, flips, and frappes with such specialties as the Chocolate Bouquet, an orange-chocolate ice cream soda, and the Strawberry Jam, a drink made with strawberry syrup and crushed berries. Catchy names enhanced the appeal of such fountain offerings as the Cherry Bon-Bon (made with cherry syrup and ice cream), the Golf Goblet (flavored with pineapple syrup, lemon juice, and raspberry vinegar), and the New York Beauty (a strawberry soda with vanilla ice cream). At least one favorite seems to have outlived the soda fountain: the Black Cow, which is, in its simplest form, a scoop of vanilla ice cream in a glass of root beer. Substitute chocolate soda and coffee ice cream and you'll have the Broadway, hugely popular during World War II.

Although ingredients like Blackberry Floss and Ginger Cordial Syrup are no longer available, you can easily re-create many old-fashioned sodas (or invent new ones) with the vast variety of soft drink and ice cream flavors on the market today. For a nostalgic finale to a summer party, set up a "soda fountain" with soft drinks, ice cream, flavored syrups, seltzer, and whipped cream. Put out tall glasses, straws, and long spoons, and let your guests take their fill of what was dubbed, in 1893, "the national beverage."

At right, some soda-fountain specials: the Cherry Bon-Bon, Chocolate Bouquet, Strawberry Jam, Broadway, New York Beauty, and Golf Goblet.

TEXAS BARBECUE

Orange Lemonade

Beer-Marinated Pepper Steaks

Grilled Vegetable Kebabs • *Country Biscuits*

Oven-Fried Potato Wedges • *Cowboy Beans*

Open-Faced Peach Pie

SERVES 16

▼

Round up a herd of friends for this down-home outdoor get-together (you can double the recipes if it's a real stampede). Texas is the land of fine beef and open-handed hospitality, and this cookout calls for thick cuts of beef and generous portions of everything else. The steaks, marinated in beer and spices, are grilled to order; for a true taste of Texas, add some mesquite wood chunks or chips to the fire.

Making the side dishes in advance will free you to concentrate on grilling the steaks and the vegetable kebabs. The potatoes and beans will stay warm in heavy, heat-holding dishes: Crockery bowls and rustic agateware pans will do the job as they underscore the Western mood. You can keep the biscuits (homemade or store-bought) toasty in a cloth-lined basket. A few innings of softball or rounds of horseshoes will keep your guests occupied until mealtime—and hone their appetites as well. Then just ring the dinner bell and watch 'em come running!

Orange Lemonade

This is a "thirsty" meal with several spicy dishes, so you'll want to provide plenty to drink. Have lots of iced beer on hand, as well as this tart juice blend. Serve the orange lemonade over crushed ice; seltzer can be added to make a fizzy drink.

6 quarts orange juice

6 cups lemon juice

6 oranges, sliced

6 lemons, sliced

1. Pour the orange and lemon juices into a large bowl and stir well.

2. Refrigerate the orange lemonade until well chilled, then add the sliced oranges and lemons. Pour some of the beverage into a large pitcher and refill as needed.

Makes about 32 cups

There's no need for paper napkins when inexpensive, easy-care cotton bandannas come in such a wide range of colors; their lap-covering size makes them most welcome at any barbecue. Tuck them into tumblers or clip them with wooden clothespins to keep them from blowing away on a breezy day.

Beer-Marinated Pepper Steaks

T-bone steaks are the first choice for this recipe, but any kind of steaks can be used as long as they are at least one inch thick. Each steak will provide about three servings, so the six steaks called for here should accommodate any larger-than-usual appetites. Adding mesquite or another fragrant wood to a barbecue fire will give the steaks a deliciously smoky savor. For more about flavoring the fire for grilling, see Savory Smoke, pages 148-149.

1½ cups beer

1½ cups bottled chili sauce

2 onions, coarsely chopped

½ cup chopped parsley

⅓ cup Dijon mustard

3 tablespoons brown sugar

2 tablespoons Worcestershire sauce

2 tablespoons paprika

1½ teaspoons dry mustard

½ teaspoon ground black pepper

Six 1½-pound steaks, preferably

*   T-bones, about 1 inch thick*

⅓ cup whole peppercorns

1. In a large glass baking dish, combine the beer, chili sauce, onions, parsley, Dijon mustard, sugar, Worcestershire sauce, paprika, dry mustard, and ground black pepper. Place the steaks in the marinade, cover with plastic wrap, and refrigerate for at least 4 hours or overnight, turning occasionally.

2. Prepare the barbecue or preheat the broiler.

3. In a mortar, or under the flat of a heavy knife blade, crush the whole peppercorns. Remove the steaks from the baking dish and discard the marinade. Sprinkle both sides of each steak with 1 tablespoon of the crushed peppercorns and press them into the meat with the heel of your hand. Place the steaks on the grilling rack or broiler pan and cook them 4 inches from the heat for 7 to 8 minutes per side (for rare), 9 to 10 minutes per side (for medium-rare), or 11 to 12 minutes per side (for well done). To serve, cut the meat from the bones and slice the steaks. *16 servings*

Grilled Vegetable Kebabs

If there isn't room on the barbecue for both the kebabs and the steaks, grill the vegetables first. They take only about ten minutes to cook and can be grilled before the fire is hot enough for the steaks. Wrap the cooked kebabs in foil to keep them warm until ready to serve. If you have wooden rather than metal skewers, soak them in water for an hour before use so that they do not scorch.

1 cup olive oil
4 cloves garlic, minced
1½ teaspoons oregano
1½ teaspoons basil
1 teaspoon salt
½ teaspoon black pepper

4 medium yellow squash, cut into
    1-inch pieces
4 medium green bell peppers, cut into
    1-inch squares
32 medium mushrooms
32 cherry tomatoes

1. Prepare the barbecue or preheat the broiler.
2. In a small bowl, stir together the oil, garlic, oregano, basil, salt, and black pepper.
3. Alternating the vegetables, arrange them on 16 metal skewers, beginning and ending each skewer with a mushroom. Brush the skewered vegetables with the olive oil mixture.
4. Grill the kebabs 4 inches from the heat, turning and basting them frequently, for about 5 minutes per side, or until the vegetables are tender.   *16 servings*

Mini-size vegetables, like the baby yellow squash, zucchini, cup-shaped Sunburst squash, Belgian carrots, and pearl onions shown here, can be substituted for cut-up vegetables when making the kebabs. The unusual circular skewers have a rustic, true-West feeling.

Oven-Fried Potato Wedges

This recipe allows for a whole potato per person. With the generous quantities of food in this menu, you will not need hefty eight-ounce potatoes—unless you want to plan for leftovers, which are delicious.

16 medium baking potatoes
1 stick (4 ounces) butter, melted
½ cup olive oil
4 cloves garlic, minced

1½ teaspoons salt
½ teaspoon pepper
1 cup grated Romano cheese

1. Preheat the oven to 400°. Line two baking sheets with foil.
2. Cut each potato lengthwise into 8 wedges.
3. Stir together the butter, olive oil, garlic, salt, and pepper.
4. Place half of the potato wedges on the prepared baking sheets and brush them with the butter mixture. Sprinkle them with half the cheese and bake, turning occasionally, for 40 minutes, or until the potatoes are browned. Transfer the cooked potatoes to a deep pan and cover them with foil to keep warm while you cook the remaining potatoes.   *16 servings*

Cowboy Beans

Only long, slow cooking can produce the wonderfully mellow, smoky flavor of this well-seasoned bean dish. Happily, the beans are simmered on the stove, not baked in the oven, so you don't have to worry about overheating the kitchen. If it suits your schedule better, you can soak the beans overnight in cold water instead of bringing them to a boil and letting them stand for an hour. In warm weather, it's a good idea to let the beans soak in the refrigerator rather than at room temperature.

1 pound dried pinto beans, rinsed and
 picked over
1 large ham hock, cut into quarters (have
 the butcher do this)
1 can (28 ounces) whole tomatoes, with
 their juice
1 can (4 ounces) chopped mild green
 chilies, drained
1 medium green bell pepper, chopped
 (about 1½ cups)

1 medium onion, chopped (about 1¼ cups)
4 cloves garlic, coarsely chopped
1 fresh jalapeño pepper, seeded and minced
⅓ cup tomato paste
¼ cup Dijon mustard
3 tablespoons brown sugar
1 teaspoon dry mustard
1 teaspoon salt
¼ teaspoon black pepper
1 bay leaf

1. Place the beans in a large saucepan with water to cover by 2 inches. Bring to a boil and boil for 2 minutes. Remove from the heat, cover, and let stand for 1 hour.

2. Drain the beans and place in a large saucepan or soup pot. Add 2 cups of water, the ham hock, canned tomatoes with their juice, the green chilies, bell pepper, onion, garlic, jalapeño, tomato paste, Dijon mustard, sugar, dry mustard, salt, black pepper, and bay leaf. Bring to a boil over medium-high heat. Reduce the heat to medium-low and simmer, partially covered, for 2 hours, stirring occasionally. Remove the cover and simmer, stirring occasionally, for 30 minutes longer.

3. Remove and discard the bay leaf. Remove the ham hock. When it is cool enough to handle, remove the meat from the bone, cut it into bite-size pieces and return the meat to the pot.

16 servings

The 1923 Motorists' Luncheon Book, a compendium of picnics, noted that "the most hunger-producing appetizer in the world is the aroma . . . of meat broiling over a campfire's glowing coals. . . . There is an art in being able to build a fire out of doors. . . there must first be built, around a slightly hollowed place, a little wall of rocks, then a brisk fire started . . . and allowed to burn fiercely until it is only a glowing bed of coals."

Beer-Marinated Pepper Steak, Grilled Vegetable Kebabs, Oven-Fried Potato Wedges, and Cowboy Beans

Open-Faced Peach Pie

The Texas hill country (northwest of San Antonio) is also peach country, where peach lovers are experts at giving the sweet, succulent fruit its due. In this recipe, the peaches are delicately spiced and baked in a bottom crust only, so that the still-warm pie seems to beg for a scoop of rich vanilla ice cream or a generous spoonful of lightly sweetened whipped cream to top it off. This pie tastes best if eaten before it cools completely, but you will hear no complaints if you serve it at room temperature. To serve sixteen people, make at least two pies.

There was always more than enough food to go around at the 19th-century Southern barbecues remembered by Martha McCulloch-Williams in her book Dishes & Beverages of the Old South. *On one memorable occasion, the quantity of extra food was such that her family carried home a fore-quarter of lamb, two watermelons, and also "a lot of splendid Indian peaches."*

PASTRY
1¼ cups flour
2 tablespoons sugar
½ teaspoon salt
4 tablespoons chilled butter, cut into pieces
3 tablespoons chilled vegetable shortening, cut into pieces
4 to 5 tablespoons ice water

FILLING
8 to 10 ripe peaches
1 tablespoon lemon juice
½ cup sugar
5 tablespoons cornstarch
2 teaspoons grated orange zest
¾ teaspoon cinnamon
¼ teaspoon salt

1. Make the pastry: In a large bowl, combine the flour, sugar, and salt. With a pastry blender or two knives, cut in the butter and shortening until the mixture resembles coarse crumbs.

2. Sprinkle 2 tablespoons of the ice water over the mixture and toss it with a fork. The dough should be just barely moistened, enough so it will hold together when it is formed into a ball. If necessary, add up to 3 tablespoons more water, 1 tablespoon at a time. Form the dough into a flat disk, wrap in plastic wrap, and refrigerate for at least 30 minutes.

3. On a lightly floured surface, roll out the dough to a 12-inch circle. Fit the dough into a 9-inch glass pie plate. Trim the overhang to an even ½ inch all the way around. Fold the overhang under and crimp the dough to form a decorative border. Prick the pastry with a fork. Place the pie shell in the freezer to chill for at least 15 minutes before baking.

4. Make the filling: Halve and pit but do not peel the peaches. Cut the peaches into ½-inch-thick slices and place them in a large bowl. Add the lemon juice and toss to coat. Add the sugar, cornstarch, orange zest, cinnamon, and salt, and toss until well mixed.

5. Preheat the oven to 425°.

6. Spoon the filling into the shell and bake for 35 to 40 minutes, or until the crust is golden; set aside to cool slightly before serving. *Makes one 9-inch pie*

Open-Faced Peach Pie

SAVORY SMOKE

For grilled foods with a unique taste, try barbecuing with natural materials that yield fragrant smoke. Although a lidded barbecue or a smoker will produce the most concentrated flavor, an open grill can be covered with a sheet of heavy foil to hold in the smoke.

Among the most popular aromatic woods are hardwoods and fruitwoods such as oak, alder, hickory, cherry, and apple. These are commonly sold in chips or chunks. To make them burn slowly and smokily, soak them in water (chips for half an hour, chunks for two hours), then place them on a wood or charcoal fire. For a gas grill, place chips in a small foil baking pan and set it on the lava rocks or on the bars above the gas jets. For electric grills, place chips in the bottom of the grill, under the heating element. Start cooking as soon as the wood begins to smoke.

Perhaps the most famous grilling wood is mesquite, a shrublike hardwood native to Mexico and the American Southwest. It is sold as chips, chunks, or natural charcoal. The charcoal imparts a milder flavor than the wood, but yields a faster, hotter flame that cooks food quickly.

Different woods complement different foods. Robust oak is best suited to ham, beef, and game, while alder is traditionally chosen for salmon and trout. Sweet, mellow hickory—a Southern favorite—is excellent for grilling pork, chicken, and turkey, as well as beef. Fruity apple and cherry woods lend a smoky sweetness to mild-flavored foods such as chicken, veal, and shellfish. The sharp flavor of mesquite is best with beef, pork, and sturdy fish steaks.

Wood is not the only natural substance that can create savory smoke. Grapevine cuttings exude a mild, winy aroma that nicely enhances poultry, fish, and shellfish. Soak the vines in water, then place them on the fire for the last ten minutes of cooking time. Corncobs (dried for a few days after the kernels are removed) produce a fragrance similar to that of hickory. And pecans, almonds, or walnuts in their shells (soak the nuts briefly after partially cracking them) add their own distinct aromas to grilled foods.

Herbs and other seasonings can also be used to scent the smoke. Soak fresh or dried herbs for half an hour before placing them on the coals: Try dill, rosemary, tarragon, or coriander. For a lively tang, toss citrus rinds, or whole spices such as cloves or cinnamon sticks, onto the coals.

Hardwoods in various forms are shown at the top of the photo (left to right): hickory chips and chunks, natural mesquite charcoal, mesquite wood chunks, and natural oak charcoal. Other flavorings for the fire: nuts, grapevines, fresh herbs, citrus rinds, and corncobs.

CAKEWALK TEA

Cream-Filled Chocolate Roulade

Orange Carrot Cake with Raisins and Walnuts

Dark Chocolate Bundt Cake

Almond Cheesecake with Chocolate Crust

Lemon-Pepper Pound Cake

Ginger Angel Food Cake with Berry Sauce

SERVES A CROWD

▼

This tea fills a summer afternoon with the fragrances of our grandmothers' baking days, and also evokes memories of the old-fashioned "cakewalk," a fund-raising event still held in some communities. One type of cake-walk resembles musical chairs: the best bakers in town contribute cakes, and the participants buy tickets to "walk" for the cakes of their choice. As music plays, the walkers march around a circle of numbered squares. When the music stops, the walkers stop; a number is drawn, and the person standing on the corresponding square wins the cake.

Encourage your guests to "walk" as well—to take a leisurely stroll around a table laden with old-fashioned cakes and a selection of hot or iced teas. A group of friends might give the tea together, each bringing one or more cakes and lending her prettiest linens and teacups. If the weather is kind, serve the tea in the garden, as shown on the cover of this book.

Cream-Filled Chocolate Roulade

This impressive dessert features a swirl of sweetened whipped cream surrounded by chocolate sponge cake. The cake portion of the recipe can be made up to 24 hours in advance and refrigerated until you are ready to fill it. To prepare the cake for storage, roll it up in a kitchen towel and let it cool as directed in Step 7. Then wrap the cake (still rolled in the towel) in a sheet of heavy-duty plastic wrap so it does not dry out. Be sure to allow ample time for the cake to return to room temperature before you fill it; if the cake is too cold, it may crack as it is rolled.

Essentials of Etiquette, published in 1924, outlined the most traditional form of late-day refreshment: "Afternoon tea, in strict etiquette, consists solely of tea, sandwiches (or hot bread) and cake. Jam or marmalade may be added, also chocolate or bouillon, and the sandwiches and the cake may be of the richest, daintiest and most varied character."

CAKE
⅓ cup sifted cake flour
¼ cup plus 2 tablespoons unsweetened cocoa powder
¼ teaspoon baking powder
¼ teaspoon salt
4 eggs, separated

1 teaspoon vanilla extract
¼ teaspoon cream of tartar
⅔ cup granulated sugar

FILLING AND GARNISH
1 cup heavy cream
¼ cup confectioners' sugar

1. Preheat the oven to 400°. Butter the bottom of a 15½ x 10½-inch jelly roll pan and line the bottom with waxed paper. Butter and flour the waxed paper.

2. Make the cake: In a medium bowl, stir together the flour, ¼ cup of the cocoa powder, the baking powder, and salt.

3. In a small bowl, beat together the egg yolks and vanilla. Stir in half of the dry ingredients.

4. In a large bowl, beat the egg whites until frothy. Add the cream of tartar and continue beating until soft peaks form. Gradually add the granulated sugar and continue beating until stiff, glossy peaks form.

5. Fold one-fourth of the beaten egg whites into the egg-yolk mixture, then fold in the remaining egg whites. Sprinkle the remaining dry ingredients over the egg mixture and gently fold them in until no streaks remain. Immediately spread the batter evenly in the prepared pan. Bake for 8 to 10 minutes, or until the top of the cake springs back when touched with your finger and a toothpick inserted in the center of the cake comes out clean and dry.

6. Lay a kitchen towel on a work surface and sift the remaining 2 tablespoons cocoa powder over it. Run a knife around the edge of the pan to loosen the cake, then turn the cake out onto the towel. Carefully peel off the waxed paper, using a sharp knife to free it if it sticks.

7. If the edges of the cake are crisp or browned, carefully trim them. Starting with one short side, roll the cake and towel together into a log. Set the rolled cake aside to cool to room temperature before filling.

8. Meanwhile, make the filling: In a medium bowl, beat the cream with 2 tablespoons of the confectioners' sugar until stiff peaks form.

9. Assemble the cake: Gently unroll the cake; do not attempt to flatten it completely. Spread the whipped cream filling evenly over the cake to within 1 inch of the edges. Starting with one short side, carefully reroll the cake, finishing with the seam side

down. Using two metal spatulas, transfer the cake to a serving platter. If not serving the cake immediately, cover it with plastic wrap and refrigerate.

10. If desired, for a neater presentation, trim a thin slice from each end of the cake.

11. Just before serving, sift the remaining 2 tablespoons confectioners' sugar over the cake.

Makes one 10-inch cake roll

Cream-Filled Chocolate Roulade

Orange Carrot Cake with Raisins and Walnuts

Vegetables have found their way into a number of American baking recipes, of which carrot cake is certainly one of the most popular. Shredded carrots give the cake moistness, sweetness, and—along with raisins and walnuts in this recipe—a pleasantly varied texture. For a whimsical touch, decorate your cake with "baby" carrots made of molded marzipan, tinted with a few drops of food coloring. Add some snippings of fresh carrot tops or dill fronds to complete the illusion.

What more appropriate flowers for a tea than tea roses? Arrange them in single-color or mixed bouquets, and float any fallen petals in shallow glass bowls of water. Place some roses around the room, as well as on the tea table.

CAKE
3 cups flour
2 teaspoons baking soda
½ teaspoon salt
2 sticks (8 ounces) butter, softened to
   room temperature
1 cup (packed) dark brown sugar
⅔ cup granulated sugar
4 eggs
4 cups grated carrots (about 4 large)
1 cup chopped walnuts
1 cup golden raisins

1 teaspoon grated orange zest
1 teaspoon vanilla extract

FROSTING
11 ounces cream cheese, softened to
   room temperature
2 sticks (8 ounces) butter, softened to
   room temperature
1 tablespoon grated orange zest
1 teaspoon vanilla extract
2½ cups sifted confectioners' sugar
Marzipan carrots, for garnish (optional)

1. Preheat the oven to 350°. Butter two 8 x 2-inch round cake pans and line the bottoms with circles of waxed paper. Butter the waxed paper, then flour the pans.

2. Make the cake: In a medium bowl, stir together the flour, baking soda, and salt.

3. In a large bowl, cream the butter and sugars until smoothly blended. Beat in the eggs, one at a time, beating well after each addition until the batter is thick and light. Add the dry ingredients and beat just until blended; do not overbeat.

4. Add the carrots, walnuts, raisins, orange zest, and vanilla, and stir until blended.

5. Spread the batter evenly in the prepared pans. Rap the pans once or twice on the counter to remove any air pockets. Bake for 35 to 40 minutes, or until the tops are golden, the cakes shrink from the sides of the pans, and a toothpick inserted in the center of the cakes comes out clean.

6. Let the cakes cool in the pans for 10 minutes, then turn them out onto a rack to cool completely before filling and frosting.

7. Meanwhile, make the frosting: In a medium bowl, beat the cream cheese and butter until smooth. Beat in the orange zest and vanilla. Gradually add the confectioners' sugar, beating well after each addition until the frosting is thick and smooth.

8. Frost the cake: Remove the waxed paper from the layers. Spread a generous layer of frosting over one cake layer. Top with the second layer, then frost the top and sides of the cake. Garnish with marzipan carrots, if desired.

Makes one 8-inch layer cake

Dark Chocolate Bundt Cake

Both cocoa powder and a full half-pound of semisweet chocolate are used to make this richer-than-devil's-food chocolate Bundt cake. A white glaze drizzled over the top helps to emphasize its fluted shape. However, if you don't have a Bundt pan, a large tube pan can be substituted.

*½ cup plus 2 tablespoons unsweetened
  cocoa powder*
*8 ounces semisweet chocolate,
  cut into pieces*
2 cups flour
1½ teaspoons baking powder
¼ teaspoon salt
*2 sticks (8 ounces) butter, softened to
  room temperature*

1½ cups (packed) brown sugar
4 eggs
1½ teaspoons vanilla extract
1 cup milk

GLAZE
¾ cup confectioners' sugar
1 tablespoon milk

1. Preheat the oven to 350°. Butter a 12-cup Bundt pan or 10-inch tube pan and dust it with 2 tablespoons of the cocoa powder.

2. Make the cake: In a double boiler, melt the chocolate over hot, not simmering, water, stirring occasionally until smooth. Set aside to cool slightly.

3. Meanwhile, in a medium bowl, stir together the flour, the remaining ½ cup cocoa, the baking powder, and salt. Set aside.

4. In a large bowl, cream the butter and brown sugar until light and fluffy. Beat in the eggs, one at a time, then beat in the vanilla. Add the melted chocolate and beat until blended.

5. Alternating between the two, gradually add the dry ingredients and the milk, beating just until blended; do not overbeat.

6. Spread the batter evenly in the prepared pan. Rap the pan once or twice on the counter to remove any air pockets. Bake for 55 to 60 minutes, or until the top of the cake springs back when touched, and a toothpick inserted in the center of the cake comes out clean and dry.

7. Let the cake cool in the pan on a rack for 15 minutes.

8. Meanwhile, make the glaze: In a small bowl, stir together the confectioners' sugar and milk until smooth and pourable.

9. Turn the cake out onto a serving dish, rounded-side up, and drizzle the glaze over the top.

Makes one 10-inch Bundt cake

It's nearly impossible to go wrong when mixing floral-patterned china teacups and pots; almost all of them go well together. Offer several types of tea: old favorites such as English Breakfast and Darjeeling as well as herbal or fruit-flavored brews.

Almond Cheesecake with Chocolate Crust

Almond Cheesecake with Chocolate Crust

The combination of ricotta, cream cheese, and almond paste makes this Italian-style cheesecake extraordinarily rich and smooth. If you'd like to serve fruit with it, cherries, peaches, or plums would nicely complement its flavor.

15 graham cracker squares
*   (about 3½ ounces)*
¼ cup butter
1 ounce semisweet chocolate,
*   cut into pieces*
½ cup chopped toasted almonds
2 cups (1 pound) ricotta cheese

1 package (8 ounces) cream cheese,
*   softened to room temperature*
1 package (8 ounces) almond paste
¼ cup sugar
3 eggs
1 teaspoon vanilla extract

1. Preheat the oven to 350°.

2. In a food processor or blender, process the graham crackers to fine crumbs; transfer the crumbs to a bowl and set aside.

3. In a small saucepan over low heat, melt the butter and chocolate, stirring until smooth. Add the chocolate mixture and the chopped almonds to the crumbs, and stir to combine, then pat the crumb mixture into the bottom and halfway up the sides of an 8½ x 2½-inch round springform pan; set aside.

4. In a medium bowl, combine the ricotta, cream cheese, and almond paste, and beat until smooth. Beat in the sugar. Add the eggs, one at a time, beating well after each addition.

5. Add the vanilla and beat until smooth. Pour the filling into the crust. Bake for 1 hour, or until the filling is golden around the edges and begins to crack in the center. Let the cake cool completely in the pan on a rack.

6. To serve, place the pan on a serving platter, run a knife around the edge of the pan and remove the rim.

Makes one 8½-inch cake

Lemon-Pepper Pound Cake

You'll taste the lemon as soon as you bite into a slice of this old-fashioned cake; the pepper's spark comes as a lively aftertaste. Be sure to use white pepper so that there are no dark flecks in the cake.

2 cups flour
¾ teaspoon baking powder
¾ teaspoon white pepper
¼ teaspoon salt
⅔ cup butter, softened to room temperature

⅔ cup sugar
3 eggs
1 teaspoon vanilla extract
2 teaspoons grated lemon zest
⅓ cup milk

1. Preheat the oven to 350°. Butter and flour an 8½-inch loaf pan.

2. In a medium bowl, stir together the flour, baking powder, pepper, and salt; set aside.

3. In a large bowl, cream the butter and sugar. Beat in the eggs, one at a time, then beat in the vanilla. Beat in the lemon zest. Alternating between the two, gradually add the dry ingredients and the milk, beating just until combined; do not overbeat.

4. Spread the batter evenly in the prepared pan. Rap the pan once or twice on the counter to remove any air pockets. Bake for 40 to 50 minutes, or until the top of the cake springs back when touched, and a toothpick inserted in the center of the cake comes out clean and dry.

5. Let the cake cool in the pan on a rack for 5 minutes, then turn it out onto the rack to cool completely.

Makes one 8-inch loaf cake

*A*nnie Gregory, author of the 1906 Blue Ribbon Cook Book, *took a fairly casual, relaxed view of the afternoon tea party: "These receptions enable all to show the spirit of hospitality, for everyone can entertain after this fashion, even though they have not the money to make a grand spread."*

Ginger Angel Food Cake with Berry Sauce

Because it is so light textured and rises so high, there seems to be a mystique about making an angel food cake. But the recipe for this cloudlike dessert is quite straightforward and should pose no difficulties for the home baker. Grated fresh ginger gives it an intriguing spiciness, which serves as a perfect foil for the accompanying three-berry sauce. Superfine sugar produces the lightest cake, but if you are unable to find it, process granulated sugar in a food processor or blender until fine but not powdered; measure the sugar again after processing.

Christine Terhune Herrick's 1902 book, **In City Tents,** *assisted young homemakers "of slender means" with suggestions such as this one: "Afternoon tea is probably the simplest fashion in which to exercise hospitality. Pretty cups and saucers are among the possessions of which the young housekeeper has a generous store, and they will make an attractive array on her afternoon tea table."*

CAKE
1 cup sifted cake flour
1¾ cups superfine sugar
*16 large egg whites (2 cups), at room
   temperature*
1 teaspoon cream of tartar
½ teaspoon salt
1 tablespoon finely grated fresh ginger
1 teaspoon vanilla extract

BERRY SAUCE
½ pint strawberries
½ pint raspberries
½ cup blueberries
2 tablespoons superfine sugar
Whipped cream (optional)

1. Preheat the oven to 350°.
2. Make the cake: Sift the flour and ½ cup of the sugar three times; set aside.
3. In a large bowl, beat the egg whites, cream of tartar, and salt until soft peaks form. Very gradually beat in 1¼ cups of sugar, then continue beating until stiff peaks form; they should look glossy, not dry.
4. Sift about ¼ cup of the dry ingredients over the beaten egg whites, then fold in, using a rubber spatula. Fold in the ginger and the vanilla, then fold in the remaining dry ingredients, ¼ cup at a time.
5. Spread the batter evenly in an ungreased 10-inch tube pan with a removable bottom. Rap the pan once on the counter to remove any air pockets. Bake for 40 minutes, or until the cake shrinks from the sides of the pan, and a toothpick inserted into the cake comes out clean.
6. Turn the pan upside down (if your pan does not have "legs," slip the tube of the pan over the neck of a bottle). Let the cake cool, upside down, for 1½ hours, then run a knife around the edge of the pan and pull off the sides of the pan. Run a knife around the tube and the bottom of the pan and turn the cake out onto a plate.
7. Make the berry sauce: Place half of the strawberries, raspberries, and blueberries in a bowl and gently mash them. Stir in the sugar, then fold in the remaining berries. Serve the cake with the berry topping, and whipped cream, if desired.

Makes one 10-inch tube cake

Ginger Angel Food Cake with Berry Sauce

A TABLETOP GARDEN

Summer is the easiest time of year to create a striking floral centerpiece. Whether you have your own cutting garden or bring home blooms from a florist's shop or farmers' market, you can easily create an arrangement that will truly bring the garden indoors.

As a change from glass or ceramic vases, consider borrowing containers and accessories from the backyard or potting shed. Watering cans, flower baskets, birdhouses, garden implements, and even small sculptures (like the cast "stone" animals shown here) can be grouped into appealing still lifes with cultivated or wild flowers. Herbs, such as dill, spearmint, and parsley, will also lend their graceful forms and heady fragrances to any summer centerpiece. A pair of gardening gloves or a weathered straw hat would add a whimsical note.

Favorite collectibles—like the cool blue-green patent-medicine bottles shown above—can form the basis for a more unified floral arrangement. Pitchers, creamers, canning jars, drinking glasses, milk bottles, or teapots also make ideal containers for large or small bouquets. Consider filling pretty teacups with water and floating a few petals on the surface. Even baskets or tins (with jars or glasses placed inside to hold water) can serve as "vases."

For long-lasting arrangements, cut flowers early in the day or late in the afternoon. Sever the stems with a sharp knife and immediately place them in a bucket of warm water. Before fashioning your arrangement, strip the stems of leaves or thorns that will lie below the water line; otherwise, as these decay, they will produce bacteria that can block the stems.

BOX SOCIAL

Honey-Pecan Chicken

Macaroni and Bell Pepper Salad

Browned-Onion Biscuits • Nasturtium Butter

Melon Cooler

Chocolate Cream Cheese Cupcakes

SERVES 4

▼

Fund-raising box socials, which combined good food and good works with a bit of romance, were popular in the late nineteenth century. Women prepared and packed meals for two; men bid for the boxes in an auction, and each winning bidder shared the meal with the woman whose "prize" he had won. A married man might play it safe and bid for his wife's dependably good food, while a bachelor might be more interested in his companion than in the quality of her cooking.

Today a "box social" picnic—minus the quaint social entanglements—can take place in a garden or at an outdoor concert. See that everything is attractively packed: line small baskets with brightly colored cloth or paper napkins, or dress up shoeboxes with giftwrap. Glossy white cake boxes, which can be purchased at most bakeries, are another possibility. Embellish each carrier with a ribbon and a tiny nosegay.

Honey-Pecan Chicken

A few hours' soaking in buttermilk, which is slightly acid, renders the chicken juicy and tender; the pecan breading seals in the succulence while the bird cooks to golden crispness. This recipe can also be made with just breasts, thighs, or drumsticks.

3-pound chicken, cut into 8 serving
   pieces, rinsed
½ cup buttermilk, or ½ cup milk plus
   1½ teaspoons vinegar
4 slices stale whole-wheat bread
1 cup pecans

¼ cup parsley sprigs
3 tablespoons butter, cut into pieces
2 cloves garlic
½ teaspoon salt
½ teaspoon pepper
¼ cup honey

   1. Place the chicken pieces in a large plastic bag, add the buttermilk, and seal the bag. Place it in a bowl and refrigerate for at least 2 hours, turning occasionally.

   2. Preheat the oven to 425°. Line a baking sheet with foil and grease the foil.

   3. Place the bread in a food processor and process to coarse crumbs. Add the pecans, parsley, butter, garlic, salt, and pepper, and pulse on and off for about 3 seconds, or until the butter is just incorporated. Transfer the breading mixture to a shallow bowl.

   4. Drain the chicken pieces, then dredge them in the breading mixture. Place the chicken pieces, skin-side up, on the prepared baking sheet, leaving space between them. Drizzle the honey over the chicken.

   5. Bake the chicken for 15 minutes, then reduce the oven temperature to 350° and bake for 30 to 35 minutes longer, or until the juices run clear when the chicken is pierced with a sharp knife.

4 servings

Macaroni and Bell Pepper Salad

Macaroni salad, an American picnic standard, is updated here. The old favorite—elbow macaroni in a mayonnaise dressing—is enlivened with tangy cider vinegar, fresh coriander, and a touch of cayenne pepper. Pack this side dish in mugs, sturdy paper cups, or covered plastic freezer containers.

2 cups elbow macaroni (about 9 ounces)
1 teaspoon vegetable oil
1 cup mayonnaise
¼ cup cider vinegar
3 tablespoons Dijon mustard
⅓ cup chopped fresh coriander
1½ teaspoons celery seeds, crushed

1 teaspoon salt
½ teaspoon black pepper
⅛ teaspoon cayenne pepper
1 cup diced green bell pepper
1 cup diced carrots
1 cup pitted small black olives

1. In a large saucepan of boiling salted water, cook the macaroni according to package directions until tender but still firm. Drain, rinse under cold running water, and drain again. Return the macaroni to the pan and toss it with the oil; set aside.

2. In a large bowl, combine the mayonnaise, vinegar, mustard, coriander, celery seeds, salt, black pepper, and cayenne, and stir until well blended.

3. Add the macaroni, bell pepper, carrots, and olives to the dressing, and toss gently until the macaroni is well coated with dressing. Cover the bowl and refrigerate the salad for at least 1 hour, or until the flavors are blended.   *4 servings*

The Box Social meal

Browned-Onion Biscuits

Caramelized onions add a mellow sweetness to these biscuits. Cutting the dough with a knife, rather than with a biscuit cutter, simplifies the preparation a bit. This recipe makes nine biscuits—two for each guest and an extra for the cook!

6 tablespoons chilled butter
½ cup chopped onion
1 teaspoon sugar
⅔ cup buttermilk, or ⅔ cup milk plus
   2 teaspoons vinegar

2 cups flour
2 teaspoons baking powder
½ teaspoon baking soda
½ teaspoon salt

1. Preheat the oven to 400°. Lightly grease a baking sheet.
2. In a small saucepan, melt 3 tablespoons of the butter over medium heat. Add the onion and sugar, and cook, stirring frequently, until the onion is golden brown, about 10 minutes. Remove the pan from the heat. When the onion is slightly cooled, stir in the buttermilk; set aside.
3. Cut the remaining 3 tablespoons butter into small pieces.
4. In a large bowl, stir together the flour, baking powder, baking soda, and salt. Using a pastry blender or two knives, cut in the butter until the mixture resembles coarse crumbs. Make a well in the center.
5. Pour the buttermilk mixture into the dry ingredients and stir briefly to form a dough. Transfer the dough to a lightly floured surface. Using a floured rolling pin, roll out the dough to a 7½-inch square. Cut the dough into nine 2½-inch squares.
6. Place the biscuits on the prepared baking sheet and bake for 20 to 25 minutes, or until golden.

Makes 9 biscuits

The **Art of Entertaining,** *published in 1927, suggested a "box party" bridge luncheon: "Take eight boxes about twelve inches square, and cover them with flowered wallpaper, having two alike. For instance, two boxes may be covered with rose wallpaper, two with flame-colored nasturtiums, two with lavender orchids, and two with yellow jonquils." Each pair of guests whose boxes matched would be partners for lunch and bridge.*

Nasturtium Butter

The delicate flavor of sweet (unsalted) butter will allow the subtle taste of the nasturtiums (which have a mild watercress flavor) to come through. Be sure the blossoms you use have not been treated with pesticides; either pick some from your own unsprayed garden, or buy the flowers at a gourmet shop or farmers' market. If nasturtiums are unavailable, blend some chopped fresh herbs into the butter.

1 stick (4 ounces) unsalted butter,
   softened to room temperature

8 nasturtium flowers

1. In a small bowl, cream the butter until very soft.
2. Place a flower against the inside of each of 4 small glass or plastic cups, then pack the butter into the cups. Place a flower on top of each cup of butter.
3. Cover each cup tightly with plastic wrap and refrigerate for at least 1 hour, or overnight.

4 servings

Melon Cooler

Melon Cooler

Lidded jelly glasses are perfect for packing single beverage servings. This recipe makes seven to eight cups. After filling one glass for each box supper, pour the remaining melon cooler into a thermos and bring it along to the picnic for refills.

4 pounds watermelon

2½ pounds cantaloupe

Small melon wedges and fresh mint leaves

for garnish (optional)

1. Remove the watermelon flesh from the rind. Seed the flesh and cut it into large cubes. Quarter the cantaloupe and cut off the rind. Cut the cantaloupe flesh into large chunks.

2. Place the watermelon and cantaloupe in a food processor or blender and process until puréed. Strain the purée into a pitcher, cover, and refrigerate until well chilled. At serving time, stir well and, if desired, garnish each glass with a skewer of melon wedges and fresh mint leaves. *4 servings*

Chocolate Cream Cheese Cupcakes

Moist and chocolaty, these cupcakes are like miniature cheesecakes. For a picnic, bake them in colorful paper or foil baking cups, then pack them in a separate container to protect the fudgy frosting. Send any extra cupcakes home with your guests.

CHOCOLATE BATTER
¾ cup flour
⅓ cup unsweetened cocoa powder
½ teaspoon baking soda
⅓ cup butter, softened to room
   temperature
⅔ cup sugar
2 eggs
½ teaspoon vanilla extract
½ cup sour cream

CREAM CHEESE BATTER
1 package (3 ounces) cream cheese,
   softened to room temperature

¼ cup sour cream
3 tablespoons sugar
1 egg
½ teaspoon vanilla extract

ICING
¼ cup sugar
¼ cup heavy cream
1 ounce semisweet chocolate,
   broken into pieces
2 tablespoons butter

The generally approved menu for a box supper (according to an account in The Country Kitchen) consisted of chicken—white meat and drumsticks only— thin slices of buttered bread, and sweet cucumber or watermelon-rind pickles. Each woman packed one or more of her dessert specialties: a thick cut of marble cake, a carefully wrapped wedge of fig layer cake with thick egg-white frosting, or a pretty slice of jelly roll.

1. Preheat the oven to 350°. Line 12 cupcake tins with paper baking cups.

2. Make the chocolate batter: In a medium bowl, stir together the flour, cocoa powder, and baking soda.

3. In a large bowl, cream the butter and sugar. Beat in the eggs, one at a time, beating well after each addition. Beat in the vanilla. Gradually beat in the sour cream, then add the dry ingredients and stir just until blended; do not overbeat. Set aside.

4. Make the cream cheese batter: In a medium bowl, beat the cream cheese with the sour cream until smooth. Beat in the sugar, egg, and vanilla. Set aside.

5. Divide the chocolate batter evenly among the cupcake tins, filling them no more than half full. Spoon the cream cheese batter on top (the cups will be filled to within ¼ inch of their tops). Bake for 20 to 25 minutes, or until the tops of the cupcakes spring back when touched with your finger. Cool the cupcakes in the pans for 5 minutes, then place them on a rack to cool completely before frosting; do not remove the paper baking cups.

6. Meanwhile, make the icing: In a small, heavy saucepan, bring the sugar and cream to a boil, stirring constantly. Reduce the heat so the mixture simmers and cook without stirring for 5 minutes.

7. Remove the pan from the heat, add the chocolate and butter, and stir until melted. Transfer the icing to a medium bowl and beat until it is smooth and spreadable and will just hold soft peaks, 7 to 10 minutes.

8. Spread a thick layer of icing on the top of each cupcake.   *Makes 12 cupcakes*

Chocolate Cream Cheese Cupcakes

Photography, Prop, and Design Credits

All photographs by Steven Mays, with the assistance of Rob Whitcomb. The Editors would like to thank the following for their contributions as designers or for their courtesy in lending items for photography. Items not listed below are privately owned. **Page 8**: Halloween ribbon—C. M. Offray & Son, Chester, NJ. **Page 13**: ceramic pumpkin and cabbage tureens—Eigen Arts, Jersey City, NJ. **Pages 20-21**: pumpkin carving executed by Ginger Hansen Shafer, NYC. **Pages 22-23**: "Mesa" blue and white bowls, salad plates, ramekins, tureen, flatware—Dansk International Designs, Mount Kisco, NY; copper pots—Charles F. Lamalle, NYC; terra-cotta crudité dish, blue glass pitcher, Mexican motif serving spoon, checked napkins—Pottery Barn, NYC; wooden candlesticks, iron cactus, wooden coyote—Distant Origin, NYC. **Page 28**: mugs, glass compotes—Pottery Barn; oval wooden Shaker serving tray—Shaker Workshops, Concord, MA. **Pages 30-31**: chilies courtesy of Oak Grove Plantation, The Blew Family, Pittstown, NJ. **Pages 32-33**: "Traviata" Ceralene dinner and salad plates, gold-edged crystal wineglasses—Baccarat, Madison Avenue, NYC; trays, napkins, woven place mats, footed glass compote—Frank McIntosh at Henri Bendel, NYC; green-handled flatware, salad serving pieces, salad bowl—Dampierre & Co., NYC. **Page 34**: napkin, lace place mat—Frank McIntosh at Henri Bendel. **Page 37**: "Traviata" Ceralene cups and saucers, dessert plates, teapot—Baccarat. **Pages 40-41**: "Evesham Gold" dinner plates, covered casserole, sauceboat and saucer, pasta bowl (holding stuffing), soup cups and saucers—Royal Worcester, NYC; soupspoon, tablecloth—Dampierre & Co., NYC; ceramic vegetable and fruit containers—Eigen Arts, Jersey City, NJ; "Leaf Stripe" wallpaper, Williamsburg adaptation—Katzenbach & Warren, NYC. **Page 42**: knife and fork—Dampierre & Co. **Page 49**: antique green majolica plates—Dampierre & Co. **Pages 50-51**: wheat sheaves designed by Ginger Hansen Shafer,

NYC; Gien animal motif dinner plates, "Montaigne Optic" wineglasses—Baccarat, Madison Avenue, NYC; brass chargers, small brass bowls with handles—Mottahedeh & Co., NYC; staghorn-handled flatware—Asprey, NYC; napkins—Frank McIntosh at Henri Bendel, NYC; bearded wheat (in smaller sheaves)—Doxie Keller Enterprises, Hutchinson, KS. **Page 52**: glass tree ornaments—Old World Christmas, Spokane, WA; gift boxes, fruit basket gift card—The Gifted Line, Sausalito, CA; ribbon—C. M. Offray & Son, Chester, NJ; candy—Bob's Candies, Albany, GA. **Pages 54-55**: black buffet plates, "Diego Mon Ami" stainless-steel flatware—Sasaki Crystal, NYC; "Black Agate" dinner plates, soup bowls, butter crock—Bennington Potters, Bennington, VT; glass salad bowl, wineglasses—Simon Pearce, NYC; "Barrocco Antico" napkins—Anichini Linea Casa, NYC; plaid blanket (on chair)—ABC Carpet & Home, NYC; sweater—L. L. Bean, Freeport, ME; copper pot—Charles F. Lamalle, NYC; votive candle holders designed and painted by Ginger Hansen Shafer, NYC; glass votive candle holders, candles—Hallmark, Kansas City, MO. **Page 59**: "Black Agate" cups and saucers—Bennington Potters. **Pages 62-63**: glass tree ornaments, nutcracker—Old World Christmas, Spokane, WA; ribbons—C. M. Offray & Son, Chester, NJ; wrapping papers—Hallmark, Kansas City, MO; Christmas and Santa gift boxes—The Gifted Line, Sausalito, CA; ruffled floral pillow, vintage fabric bandboxes—A Touch of Ivy, NYC; mugs—Pottery Barn, NYC; wineglasses—Dampierre & Co., NYC; Oriental rug—ABC Carpet & Home, NYC; candy canes—Bob's Candies, Albany, GA. **Page 64**: "Coffee Bean" napkins—Le Jacquard Français/Palais Royal, Charlottesville, VA. **Page 67**: "Tartan" dinner plates—Sasaki Crystal, NYC; napkins—Anichini Linea Casa, NYC; napkin rings—Dampierre & Co.; angel and fruit basket gift cards—The Gifted Line; gold ribbon—C. M. Offray & Son. **Page 68**: French horn ornament—Hallmark. **Pages**

70-71: ribbons—C. M. Offray & Son, Chester, NJ; sponged cookies decorated by Ginger Hansen Shafer, NYC. **Pages 72-73**: "Antique Roman" 24k-gold-trimmed glass dinner plates, salad plates (under bread-and-butter plates), square plates (holding salad)—Annieglass Studio, Santa Cruz, CA; "Windsor Black" porcelain bread-and-butter plates—Wedgwood, Wall, NJ; "Barrocco Nuovo" napkins—Anichini Linea Casa, NYC; bronze flatware—Zona, NYC; "Hawthorne" crystal champagne saucers—Sasaki Crystal, NYC; gold shell butter dish—Charles F. Lamalle, NYC. **Page 74**: fluted champagne glass with gold ball stem, linens, tray—Thaxton & Co., NYC; all other champagne glasses—Baccarat, Madison Avenue, NYC. **Page 77**: "Windsor Black" porcelain dessert plates—Wedgwood; Florentine tray, bronze dessert spoons—Zona; demitasse cups and saucers—Pottery Barn, NYC; gold porcelain ramekin, sugar bowl, Melior coffeepot—Charles F. Lamalle; glass fruit compote—Simon Pearce, NYC. **Page 78**: centerpiece designed by Ginger Hansen Shafer, NYC; Shaker apple basket—Shaker Workshop, Concord, MA; ribbon—C. M. Offray & Son, Chester, NJ; oval mirror—ABC Carpet & Home, NYC. **Pages 80-81**: "Fleur de Lys Blue" dinner and salad plates, platter—Spode, East Brunswick, NJ; napkins, tassel napkin rings—Pottery Barn, NYC; paisley fabric used as tablecloth—Hinson & Co., NYC. **Pages 86-87**: antique silver flatware, numbers 5, 14, and 18—Fortunoff, NYC; all other pieces—Steven E. Coulter, Des Moines, IA; lace tablecloth—ABC Carpet & Home, NYC. **Page 88**: masks, beads, doubloons—Blaine Kern Artists, New Orleans, LA; Easter eggs designed by Ginger Hansen Shafer, NYC; jacquard tablecloth—Le Jacquard Français/Palais Royal, Charlottesville, VA. **Pages 90-91**: dinner plates, soup bowls, coffee cups and saucers, soupspoons, rectangular ceramic crock, enamel pan—Fishs Eddy, NYC; masks, beads, doubloons—Blaine Kern Artists, New Orleans. **Page 93**: ceramic bowl—Fishs Eddy. **Page 97**: coffee cups, dessert plates, creamer, sugar bowl—Fishs Eddy. **Pages 98-99**: invitations executed by Ginger Hansen Shafer, NYC. **Pages 100-101**: "Pescara" soup bowls—Villeroy & Boch Tableware, NYC; "Ferrat Lace" blue buffet plates, "Marli" blue serving bowl, "Gascogne" champagne flutes—Solanée, NYC; glass caviar dish, fish napkin rings, salt and pepper shakers—Thaxton & Co., NYC; "Oceanside" salad plates, creamer—Wedgwood, Wall, NJ; silver-plated flatware—Frank McIntosh at Henri Bendel, NYC; "Brant Point Stripe" napkin fabric, "On Island" tablecloth fabric—The Nantucket Collection, Waverly Fabrics, NYC; porcelain menu—Charles F. Lamalle, NYC. **Page 103**: white porcelain tureen—Charles F. Lamalle; "Oppio" scalloped napkin—Anichini Linea Casa, NYC. **Page 105**: tray, cotton napkins, decanter, candy dish, glasses—Thaxton & Co. **Page 106**: fruit motif dessert plates, daisy cups and saucers, teapot, floral cloth, pie server—Dampierre & Co., NYC. **Page 108**: topiaries designed by Ginger Hansen Shafer, NYC; pink-trimmed cachepot, white fluted planter—Mottahedeh & Co., NYC; "Festivité" Ceralene dinner, salad, bread-and-butter plates—Baccarat, Madison Avenue, NYC; chairs—ABC Carpet & Home, NYC; napkins—Frank McIntosh at Henri Bendel, NYC. **Pages 110-111**: "Regency Pink" dinner plates, cups and saucers, "Hana" wineglasses—Sasaki Crystal, NYC; blue-and-white sponged platter, egg cup (holding strawberry butter), serving bowl—Bennington Potters, Bennington, VT; Easter eggs decorated by Ginger Hansen Shafer, NYC; "Bouquet" turquoise tablecloth—Le Jacquard Français/Palais Royal, Charlottes-ville, VA. **Page 114**: pink-and-white sponged creamer—Bennington Potters. **Pages 116-117**: plaid napkin—ABC Carpet & Home, NYC; tiles—American Olean Tile Co., Landsdale, PA. **Pages 118-119**: rectangular baking dish, terra-cotta bowl, round geometric-patterned serving plates, Shaker boxes, batter bowl (holding chips), pitcher, stemware, napkins, cactus napkin holder, rug (used as tablecloth)—Pottery Barn, NYC. **Pages 124-125**: cactus pots and gift-wrapping designed by Ginger Hansen Shafer, NYC. **Page 126**: pink, red, yellow napkins, terra-cotta containers, candlesticks, Mexican glasses—ABC Carpet & Home, NYC; tin tray, striped napkins, turquoise table runner—Pan American Phoenix, NYC; "silver" plates—Wilton Armetale, NYC; turquoise napkin, forks, cake knife—Pottery Barn, NYC; lacquer tray—Frank McIntosh at Henri Bendel, NYC. **Page 127**: laminated countertop—Formica Corp., Wayne, NJ, also available at Manhattan Laminates, NYC. **Pages 130-131**: red buffet plates—Sasaki Crystal, NYC; "Wedgwood White" dinner plates—Wedgwood, Wall, NJ; glass bowls—Pottery Barn, NYC; glass pitcher and tumblers, napkins—Simon Pearce, NYC; blue-handled flatware—Dampierre & Co., NYC. **Page 132**: sponged flowerpots decorated by Ginger Hansen Shafer, NYC. **Page 134**: glass serving bowls—Simon Pearce. **Pages 138-139**: wallcovering—Raintree Designs, NYC; clear sundae glasses on shelf, bell-shaped soda glass (center)—Libbey Glass, Toledo, OH; old-fashioned scoop, heart-shaped spoons, framed ice cream advertisement, pewter glass holder (center)—collection of Angela and Tom Sarro, Brooklyn, NY; framing—Phyllis Wrynn, Park Slope Framing, Brooklyn, NY. **Pages 140-141**: tablecloth fabric—Souleiado, available at Pierre Deux, NYC; "Black Marble" and "Blue Marble" enamel dinner plates, roasting pan, basin (holding peaches), serving spoon—CGS International, Danville, CA; "Alpha" stainless-steel flatware—Dansk International Designs, Mount Kisco, NY; glasses—Libbey Glass, Toledo, OH; deck chair, #74-368852, beechwood table, #74-368894, watermelon basket, #74-85076, galvanized steel flower bucket, #74-85076—Gardener's Eden catalog, San Francisco, CA; "One-Touch" barbecue kettle—Weber-Stephen Products Co., Palatine, IL. **Page 147**: sponged bowl (holding peaches)—Simon Pearce, NYC. **Pages 148-149**: grilling wood and charcoal—Woodchuck Cooking Wood Packaging Co., NYC, The Barbecue Industry Association, and Weber-Stephen Products Co., Palatine, IL; barbecue gloves, fork, spatula—Williams-Sonoma, San Francisco, CA; barbecue tongs—Weber-Stephen Products Co.; grill—Fortunoff Backyard Store, Westbury, NY. **Pages 150-151**: wallpaper—Hinson & Co., NYC; white lace tablecloth and napkins—paper white, ltd., Fairfax, CA. **Pages 162-163**: enamel dinner plates, mugs—Dampierre & Co., NYC; laundry basket, #W631, herb-gathering basket, #W581—Shaker Workshop, Concord, MA; croquet set—Pottery Barn, NYC; blue-and-white and pink-and-white napkins—Frank McIntosh at Henri Bendel, NYC; blue patchwork quilt, pink-and-white patchwork quilt—Thos. K. Woodard, American Antiques and Quilts, NYC.

Index

Acknowledgments

Our thanks to Dave DeWitt, Stephanie Richardson of Myers Communicounsel, Inc., Harold and Joyce Screen, and Dee Shapiro for their help on this book. Microwave oven courtesy of Litton Microwave Cooking Products. CleanTop range courtesy of the Whirlpool Corporation.

First printing
Published simultaneously in Canada
School and library distribution by Silver Burdett Company, Morristown, New Jersey

TIME-LIFE is a trademark of Time Incorporated U.S.A.

Production by Giga Communications, Inc.
Printed in U.S.A.

Library of Congress Cataloging-in-Publication Data

Country entertaining
p.   cm. — (American country)
Includes index
ISBN 0-8094-6804-2 — ISBN 0-8094-6805-0 (lib. bdg.)
1. Entertaining. 2. Cookery, American.
I. Time-Life Books.   II. Series.
TX731.C68   1991   642'.4—dc20   90-41719
CIP

American Country was created by Rebus, Inc., and published by Time-Life Books.

REBUS, INC.

Publisher: RODNEY FRIEDMAN • Editor: MARYA DALRYMPLE
Executive Editor: RACHEL D. CARLEY • Managing Editor: BRENDA SAVARD • Consulting Editor: CHARLES L. MEE, JR.
Copy Editor: ALEXA RIPLEY BARRE • Writers: JUDITH CRESSY, ROSEMARY G. RENNICKE
Design Editors: NANCY MERNIT, CATHRYN SCHWING • Contributing Editor: ANNE MOFFAT

Art Director: JUDITH HENRY • Associate Art Director: SARA REYNOLDS
Designers: AMY BERNIKER, TIMOTHY JEFFS
Photographer: STEVEN MAYS • Photo Editor: SUE ISRAEL
Photo Assistant: ROB WHITCOMB • Set Carpenter: MARCOS SORENSEN

Series Consultants: BOB CAHN, HELAINE W. FENDELMAN, LINDA C. FRANKLIN, GLORIA GALE,
KATHLEEN EAGEN JOHNSON, JUNE SPRIGG, CLAIRE WHITCOMB

Staff for *Country Entertaining*
Editor: BONNIE J. SLOTNICK
Senior Editor: NANCY MERNIT • Consulting Editor: KATE SLATE
Test Kitchen Director/Food Stylist: GRACE YOUNG WIERTZ
Test Kitchen Associate: MARIE BAKER-LEE
Copy Editor: MARSHA LUTCH LLOYD • Assistant Design Editor: LEE CUTRONE
Contributing Editor: DEE SHAPIRO
Photographer: STEVEN MAYS • Photo Assistant: ROB WHITCOMB
Freelance Food Stylist: KAREN HATT

Time-Life Books Inc. is a wholly owned subsidiary of THE TIME INC. BOOK COMPANY.

TIME-LIFE BOOKS INC.

Managing Editor: THOMAS H. FLAHERTY
Director of Editorial Resources: ELISE D. RITTER-CLOUGH
Director of Photography and Research: JOHN CONRAD WEISER
Editorial Board: DALE M. BROWN, ROBERTA CONLAN, LAURA FOREMAN, LEE HASSIG,
JIM HICKS, BLAINE MARSHALL, RITA THIEVON MULLIN, HENRY WOODHEAD

Publisher: JOSEPH J. WARD

Associate Publisher: TREVOR LUNN • Editorial Director: DONIA STEELE
Marketing Director: REGINA HALL • Director of Design: LOUIS KLEIN
Production Manager: MARLENE ZACK • Supervisor of Quality Control: JAMES KING

For information about any Time-Life book please call 1-800-621-7026, or write:
Reader Information, Time-Life Customer Service
P.O. Box C-32068, Richmond, Virginia 23261-2068